MARIEBELLE'S
ODE TO CHOCOLAT

———————

She stared with puzzlement at her treasured book

She can't help but wonder

what the story inside is all about . . .

She flips open the cover.

To her surprise she sees a mysterious dark slab

with a rich golden chandelier

As though she had entered a Palace

How amazing!!!

He contemplated her with joy.

She closed her eyes as if

she was going into a trance.

He was the man she loved,

but at that moment he took a second place.

People warned her that one

becomes a prisoner of obsession.

She held the slab and took a first bite.

Melting cream in her mouth, she screamed:

"OH. . . . CHOCOLAT!!"

MarieBelle
Entertains

MarieBelle Entertains

Savory and Sweet Recipes
for Every Occasion from the
Master Chocolatier

MARIBEL LIEBERMAN

Text by Lavinia Branca Snyder
Photography by Mark Roskams

RIZZOLI
NEW YORK

New York · Paris · London · Milan

Contents

PREFACE . . . 7

Chocolate
When Myth Becomes History . . . 9

Cacao's Long Journey
From Ancient Forest
to Modern Kitchen . . . 12

Becoming MarieBelle . . . 14

**CHOCOLATE
CREATIONS** . . . 16

IN HONDURAS . . . 34
A Garden Breakfast . . . 40
An Island Lunch . . . 48
A Never-Ending Journey . . . 56
Picnic by the Beach . . . 58
Tropical Harvest Supper . . . 66

IN AMERICA . . . 76
New York Sunday Brunch . . . 82
A Lofty Meal . . . 86
Lunch on a Terrace . . . 90
Jacques Lieberman . . . 96
Dining in Locust Valley . . . 98
A White Satin Evening . . . 108

IN SPAIN . . . 116
Of Chocolate and Traditions . . . 122
Within White Walls . . . 126
A Late Summer Celebration . . . 132
Picnic for an Afternoon Sail . . . 138
Of Tapas and Menorca . . . 144
A Fisherman's Feast . . . 150
The Gift of Chocolate . . . 158
A Sunset Supper . . . 160
Dining with Legends . . . 166

IN FRANCE . . . 174
A Light Supper in the
Shade of a Grand Allée . . . 180
French at Heart . . . 186
Dinner in Provence . . . 188
A Feast of Many Colors . . . 194

IN ITALY . . . 200
The Time Traveler . . . 206
A Table with a View . . . 210
Italian Excellence . . . 218
Dining by the Lake . . . 220
On the Santa Margherita Shore . . . 226

MARIBEL'S WORLD . . . 232
ACKNOWLEDGMENTS . . . 234
RECIPE INDEX . . . 236

Preface

The freedom to roam the world and the freedom to create—these are the treasures I am so grateful for. I am also grateful to my native Honduras, to my friends, to my parents and, most of all, to my husband and daughter. I hope that my book gives the reader a sense of all the beauty I have been gifted.

For all of us chocolate lovers, I have included the story of my native Honduras and the Lenca people; the legends and history of chocolate; how chocolate came to be a global obsession; and the process that transforms the raw cacao bean into chocolate confections.

The chapters, the anecdotes, the recipes, and the menus I share in this book are an expression of the immense joy I have received from the people and places I love. Setting a table and inviting friends to share a meal with me is the best way I know to show my gratitude for the joy they give me. I love cooking traditional dishes, but of course, be it in Spain, in France, or in Italy, there is always a little of my Honduras in all my recipes.

Table decorations are my way of extending art onto the table. At times elegant and refined and at other times filled with childish whimsy, at times historically inspired and at other times completely modern—the sense of place and occasion is what guides the mood that I reflect on my tables.

I hope you will enjoy seeing these settings, and preparing the easy-to-make recipes that follow. They are the expression of my gratitude for a wonderful and always surprising life.

CHOCOLATE
When Myth Becomes History

As a young girl growing up in Jutiquile, in the Olancho region of Honduras, future chocolatier Maribel Lieberman heard myths and stories of the Lenca people. She recalled, "Before the Spanish conquest of Honduras, the area was inhabited by a diverse population. Ethnic groups had lived in the region for millennia. One of those people were the Lenca. They were my ancestors."

And there was one Lencan myth in particular that stayed with young Maribel. She said, "The story about cacao is the one that struck me the most. It was passed down through generations of our ancestors. A legend that has yet to be entirely disproven. It goes like this: It is said that a goddess created the human race. That she descended to Earth from a far-away star. That she brought to Earth the dust from the stars, as well as cocoa powder and maize. That she mixed the three, and that is how the human being came to be. So, as you can imagine, chocolate has always been very special to me."

Recent archaeological finds in the Ulúa Valley in northern Honduras—and the analysis of chemical residue found inside ceramic vessels—provide scientific proof of the consumption of a cacao beverage in the region dating back to 1100 BCE. Everywhere you look in the Honduran countryside, whether wandering in the Mayan ruins of Copán or through the Lencan sites of Yarumela El Chircal and Tenampúa, the past is never far away.

Opposite: A carved wall of the ball court in the Mayan ruins of Copán featuring the head of a macaw. Above: Stela M, showing the Mayan ruler K'ak' Yipyaj Chan K'awiil, in front of a hieroglyphic stairway of 2,200 glyphs built in the eighth century.

The belief that led the cacao bean to become such a powerful symbol and saw it consumed ritualistically in the form of a bitter drink and prized by the Lenca elite descends from even more ancient Mesoamerican legends.

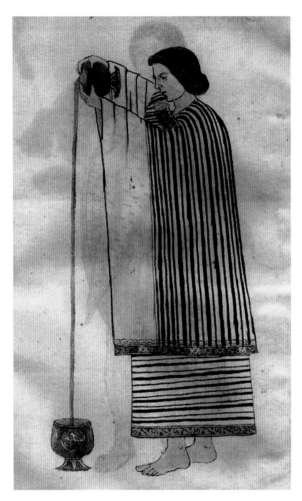

These myths were passed down through generations and transported over hundreds of miles by the Olmecs beginning in 1500 BCE and later echoed in the Mayan and Toltec cultures. In fact, cacao myths and the word *kakau* are found carved in the magnificent religious and administrative structures of the ancient cities that dot the region.

The Western word *cacao* is derived from *kakau*. The Olmecs (the earliest major civilization in Mesoamerica) lived in the lowlands of the eastern Mexican Gulf Coast and cultivated cacao trees. They believed that the feathered serpent god Quetzalcoatl had gifted the *kakau* tree to humanity. That is why they came to revere the tree, which meant nurturing it and consuming its seeds as part of their most important rituals. Subsequent civilizations, including Mayans and Toltecs, also worshipped the tree and the god who had provided it.

The Mayans made a drink called *xocolatl*, the drink of the gods. As depicted in a drawing in the 1553 manuscript known as the *Codex Tudela*, a Mayan woman ritually prepared xocolatl, making it foamy by pouring it repeatedly, and from a great height, from one vessel into another. When asked about this practice and its impact on her, Maribel smiled and said, "I have no doubt that I owe both my Cocoa Bar inspiration and the passion I feel toward my chocolate drink to these women and to their ancient ritual."

In 1325, the Aztecs conquered the Toltecs, and two centuries later they were still worshipping Quetzalcoatl, the feathered serpent god for the cacao tree and called him "the god of light, the giver of the drink of the gods, chocolate." Similar to the Mayans, the Aztecs ritualistically prepared a frothy drink made with ground cocoa beans and incorporating spices. The Aztecs called this prized drink *cacahuatl*, meaning bitter water. Cacahuatl was considered an aphrodisiac, as well as a source of physical strength that was served to warriors to prepare them for combat.

In 1502, on his fourth and final trip to the New World, Christopher Columbus claimed territory that is now Honduras for the king of Spain. He is believed to have encountered *kakau* at that time. When Columbus landed on Guanaja, one of the Bay Islands, he witnessed native inhabitants working frenetically to gather up some large seeds that had spilled in a boat. Columbus thought they were almonds, but they turned out to be cacao beans. To this day, the debate continues as to whether cacao was first brought to Spain by Columbus at that time, by conquistador Hernán Cortés in 1541, or by a group of monks in 1544.

The long history of cultivation of the cocoa bean, the mystical stories of its preparation, and reports of its medicinal properties were received by the Spanish court with great curiosity. In the decades that followed, numerous treatises were published that recounted the agricultural, geographical, and nutritional aspects of cacao.

Soon after the Spanish began importing cacao, they began sweetening the drink made with the exotic beans with sugar and incorporating cinnamon and ground almonds as well. The popularity of this "remedy" grew, and in time evolved into an increasingly popular luxurious libation, and a century later, hot chocolate had earned its place alongside coffee and tea as a high-end beverage.

In the 1753 tome *Species Plantarum*, Swedish botanist Carl Linnaeus gave the cacao tree the scientific name Theobroma cacao, or "food of the Gods." By preserving the phonetic "kakau" and adding Theobroma, he enshrined for the ages its long history and gave homage to the ancient people who first cultivated the prized bean. With the advent of the Industrial Revolution in the nineteenth century, chocolates began to be mass-produced and became widely available to everyone.

Today, the appeal of chocolate is global; and, as Maribel says, "Cacao is truly the harvest that connects us all."

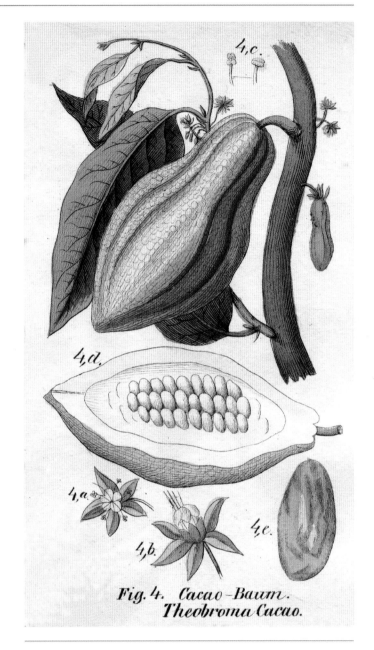

Fig. 4. Cacao-Baum. Theobroma Cacao.

Opposite, clockwise from top: *Drawing from the 1553 Codex Tudela depicting the xocolatl ritual. Quetzacoatl—the legendary feathered serpent. Ancient Mayan glyph that describes the fruit pronounced kah-kah-oo.* **Above:** *Botanical illustration of the Theobroma cacao flower, foliage, and seed pods.*

CACAO'S LONG JOURNEY
From Ancient Forest to Modern Kitchen

In her quest to produce the finest chocolates, Maribel emphasizes careful selection of raw materials. She searches for cacao pods from small farms and pays heed to ethical sourcing, ensuring that her creations are the best that they can be. "I need to bring the best beans to our chocolate, and see myself as the spokesperson of Honduran cocoa beans," Maribel told *Confectionery News*. Her chocolate products are handmade using the prized criollo bean, the highest quality single-origin cacao.

Maribel's collection of sweet confections now includes some 100 original creations. All reflect respect for culinary traditions, bold artistic vision, and wildly romantic inspiration. "I am passionate about creating new chocolate flavors, and I'm driven by gratitude at having mastered the complex culinary voyage that took me from bean to chocolate," Maribel said.

Under Maribel's watchful eye, cacao pods are carefully selected and harvested. Honduras, like other tropical areas in the Americas and Africa, is blessed with the ideal climate for growing cacao. According to the CDAIS (Capacity Development for Agricultural Innovation Systems) Honduras 2018 study, "A Story of Change on Cacao," an estimated 80 percent of Honduras's 4,000 cacao producers grow their harvests on fewer than 2.5 acres of land. Maribel said, "The country's annual production is about fifteen hundred tons, although only about ten percent of this production is deemed high quality."

The cacao pod is ready to be picked once it turns a bright yellow-orange color. The inside of a cacao pod reveals rows of beans coated in white pulp (*baba*). The beans are then cleaned, but the baba is left in place, as it aids in the next step—fermentation. Maribel said, "Cacao pods have a distinctly tropical look. Their skin is similar to that of a papaya, while their shape resembles a starfruit. The flesh is white like that of a mangosteen."

After approximately one week of fermentation, the beans begin to turn dark brown and look more like what we think of as cocoa beans. They are dried for one to two weeks, then sorted and weighed, and finally shipped to the chocolate maker.

The bean is thoroughly transformed by this process—so much so that its name changes. We refer to the pods and the raw beans as cacao, as they come from the cacao tree, but after fermentation, the beans are renamed cocoa beans. They are roasted, and their shells are removed.

The "nib"—the flesh of the cocoa bean—is then ground into cocoa mass, also known as cocoa liquor. High pressure is applied to this paste, and it separates into two distinct products: cocoa powder and cocoa butter.

Depending on its final destination, cocoa powder may be flavored with sugar and frequently vanilla. Spices like saffron or cardamom may also be added. Then the cocoa butter is reintroduced. To make milk chocolate, milk is incorporated at this point.

Not only is eating chocolate pleasurable, it is likely good for us as well. In the *American Journal of Clinical Nutrition*, Caleb J. Kelly reported that tests revealed the physiological effects of consuming cacao to be in keeping with ancient myths about its potency.

Theobromine, the primary alkaline in cocoa and chocolate, is a potent vasodilator as well as a myocardial heart stimulant. It lowers blood pressure and may help those with asthma and arteriosclerosis. (It is, however, toxic for dogs—the reason veterinarians caution against feeding chocolate to canines.)

Most people would probably agree, though, that chocolate's most enjoyable physiological qualities are its sensuous texture (because the melting point of cocoa butter is the same as the temperature of the human body, we experience it dissolving in our mouths) and the stimulant it contains, which is similar to dopamine and adrenaline. In other words, eating chocolate provides the same hormonal effects that we feel when falling in love.

Maribel said, "Setting aside the joy of the way it tastes, if we only experience a few of these effects, it is no wonder that the food of the gods has been around for thousands of years and has been called the New World's greatest gift to civilization. I am truly in awe of this culinary legacy. I am deeply grateful to my ancestors, the ancient people of Mesoamerica, for their wisdom and their gift."

Above: From cacao pods (left) to truffles tossed in cocoa powder (right).

Becoming MarieBelle

When Maribel was a child, chocolate was a popular Honduran treat, and cacao fields provided work to many in her community. Maribel herself made sweets and sold them to her friends and neighbors. Her father owned a farm, and her mother ran a boardinghouse in Jutiquile and worked as a seamstress.

One of nine siblings, Maribel still credits her close relationship with her family—and their work ethic—for her great success. "I could hear both my mother and my grandmother guiding me as I imagined what step I wanted to take next. My family taught me so much about passion and perseverance, and about wonderful food," Maribel said.

When Maribel was a teenager, her mother suggested that she enroll in secretarial courses. She gave it a valiant try, but fortunately for the world of chocolates, office work was not a good fit for Maribel. She was more of a creative and curious soul. Once she understood that about herself, there was no stopping her, and like so many before her, she emigrated from Honduras to the United States.

Living, studying, and creating in New York City made her dreams come true. She honed her creative skills and her identity at Parsons School of Design, where she explored her interest in luxury goods, design, and fashion.

Upon graduating from Parsons, Maribel found work in the fashion industry. But she still felt as though something was missing. "I felt very empty," she said. "I like fashion, but the industry is very competitive. Everybody wants to make it to the top, no matter what."

For Maribel, cooking had always been a creative outlet. So she left the fashion industry and launched the catering company Maribel's Gourmet Cuisine.

In 2000, Maribel and her best friend, Selima Salaun, opened Lunettes et Chocolat in New York's SoHo neighborhood, joining forces to reach their goals while each pursued her own individual passion. Maribel recalled, "More than a few business skeptics wondered how long an eclectic boutique offering designer eyewear and handmade chocolates could survive." The chic yet unpretentious store and its original concept built buzz immediately. Within a year, Maribel opened her Broome Street flagship boutique, MarieBelle New York. She was the first chocolatier to call the streets of SoHo home, and her imaginative culinary creations were a runaway hit.

The brand's signature ganache chocolates are handcrafted from the finest ingredients, including cacao sourced in Honduras, Colombia, and Venezuela. Maribel buys cacao directly from producers because she believes that provenance is key to both the taste and the texture of her chocolates. She also emphasizes buying from women-owned farms. She produces her single-source chocolate bars using beans from the northern region of Honduras.

"Many people are not aware that Honduras is the country where Europeans discovered people were processing cocoa beans," Maribel said.

With an appetite for growing her business, Maribel unveiled a store in Kyoto, Japan, in 2013. The opening of that first store in Japan was the culmination of her company's creative arc and the beginning of her most successful business chapter.

Today, after more than two decades, MarieBelle has an expanding global presence with two locations in New York City, a boutique at the Kitano Hotel in addition to the flagship store; three stores in Japan; and an online store in Hong Kong. From a small rural community in Honduras to New York City to a global network of retail stores, Maribel, through her company, MarieBelle, continues on her creative journey, sharing the riches of her ancient Lencan lineage.

Above, left to right: Maribel Lieberman in her MarieBelle SoHo shop. MarieBelle's signature hot chocolate and teas.

CHOCOLATE CREATIONS

MarieBelle chocolates are the expression of a young girl's dream. Hatched in her mother's kitchen in Jutiquile when she was just a child, this dream reverberates through all that Maribel Lieberman has accomplished since leaving her home in Honduras.

Maribel's chocolate creations are a gift. Through them she shares her art from the Americas to Asia. Years of painstaking work go into each perfect bite, from truffles to brownies, toffee, and caramel. The MarieBelle boutiques also pay homage to the roots of chocolate production with rich hot chocolate. The signature elaborately decorated ganache chocolates are as eye-catching as they are delicious. You'd need an atelier of your own to craft the kind of masterpieces displayed at the MarieBelle counters, but with the recipes in this chapter you can offer your guests versions of these treats that reflect the same care—and the same creative flair.

MarieBelle's Hot Chocolate

MarieBelle Aztec Hot Chocolate is made with 60% single-origin pure chocolate, resulting in a drink that is richer and has a more pronounced flavor. For American-style hot chocolate, use any kind of milk—including vegan options—or, for European-style hot chocolate, go with water.

American-style Aztec Hot Chocolate

• SERVES 2 TO 4 •

2 cups (480 ml) milk

1⅓ cups (170 g) MarieBelle Aztec Hot Chocolate

In a small saucepan, bring the milk to a simmer over medium heat.

Add the MarieBelle Aztec Hot Chocolate and whisk until dissolved and well combined. Bring to a slow boil, whisking constantly and being sure to reach the contents at the bottom of the pan to prevent the chocolate from sticking, about 30 seconds.

Pour into espresso cups or mugs and serve.

European-style Aztec Hot Chocolate

• SERVES 2 TO 4 •

1 cup (240 ml) water

1⅓ cups (170 g) MarieBelle Aztec Hot Chocolate

In a small saucepan, bring the water to a simmer over medium heat.

Add the MarieBelle Aztec Hot Chocolate and whisk until dissolved and well combined. Bring to a slow boil, whisking constantly and being sure to reach the contents at the bottom of the pan to prevent the chocolate from sticking, about 10 seconds.

Pour into espresso cups or mugs and serve.

Dark Chocolate Truffles

The secret to crafting truffles, stars of the chocolate universe, is choosing top-quality cocoa powder and chocolate. Even if I've already served a cake or cookies at the end of a meal, I like to pass around a small plate of confections with coffee and after-dinner drinks.

• MAKES ABOUT 40 TRUFFLES •

6⅓ ounces (180 g) 64% dark chocolate, roughly chopped

4⅓ ounces (120 g) 38% milk chocolate, roughly chopped

⅔ cup (160 ml) heavy cream

2 tablespoons plus 1 teaspoon (45 g) inverted sugar (see Note) or light corn syrup

3½ tablespoons (50 g) unsalted butter, at room temperature

½ cup (60 g) cocoa powder

In the top of a double boiler (or a heatproof bowl set over a pot of simmering water), combine the dark and milk chocolates and cook over simmering water, stirring occasionally, until they start to melt. Remove the chocolate from the heat before fully melted. Continue to stir until melted and smooth.

In a small saucepan, combine the heavy cream and inverted sugar and place over medium heat until the mixture comes to a boil. Remove the saucepan from the heat and pour the cream mixture over the chocolate. Stir to combine. Add the butter and stir until completely melted and smooth.

Let the mixture cool at room temperature until set but not hard, about 30 minutes.

Transfer the mixture to a pastry bag fitted with a ½-inch (12-mm) smooth tip. Pipe spheres of chocolate about ¾ inch (2 cm) in diameter onto a parchment-lined baking sheet. Refrigerate for 1 hour.

Put the cocoa powder on a plate. Gently toss the truffles in the cocoa powder to coat.

Serve immediately, refrigerate for up to 2 weeks, or freeze in an airtight container for up to 3 months. Defrost frozen truffles in the refrigerator for 24 hours, and always bring truffles to room temperature before serving.

Note: Inverted sugar is a mixture of glucose and sucrose. It is sweeter than white sugar and helps produce a smooth texture in desserts. It can be purchased online and at pastry supply stores.

Matcha Truffles

Matcha is green tea stone-ground into fine powder. Most of it is grown and prepared in Japan, specifically Kyoto and Nishio, since they both offer ideal, weather conditions.

• MAKES ABOUT 40 TRUFFLES •

13 ounces (370 g) 33% white chocolate, chopped

⅓ cup (80 ml) heavy cream

1 tablespoon (20 g) inverted sugar (see Note, page 21) or light corn syrup

3 tablespoons (45 g) unsalted butter, at room temperature

1 cup plus 2 tablespoons (90 g) matcha powder

In the top of a double boiler (or a heatproof bowl set over a pot of simmering water), melt the chocolate just until softened, stirring occasionally. Stir off the heat until melted and smooth.

In a small saucepan, combine the cream and inverted sugar and bring to a simmer over medium heat. Remove the saucepan from the heat and pour over the chocolate. Stir to combine. Add the butter and stir until smooth.

Add 2 tablespoons (10 g) of the matcha power to the chocolate mixture and stir until incorporated.

Let the mixture cool at room temperature until set but not hard, about 30 minutes.

Transfer the mixture to a pastry bag fitted with a ½-inch (12-mm) smooth tip. Pipe spheres of chocolate about ¾ inch (2 cm) in diameter onto a parchment-lined baking sheet. Refrigerate for 1 hour.

Put the remaining 1 cup (80 g) matcha powder on a plate. Roll the truffles in the matcha powder.

Serve immediately, refrigerate for up to 2 weeks, or freeze in an airtight container for up to 3 months. Defrost frozen truffles in the refrigerator for 24 hours, and always bring truffles to room temperature before serving.

Chocolate-Covered Toffee Bites

The English word caramel comes from the French, who borrowed it from the Spanish—or possibly from the Portuguese. No matter the etymology, the caramel sauce on these crunchy melt-in-your-mouth treats adds another dimension.

• MAKES ABOUT 1 POUND •

1²/₃ cups (325 g) sugar

2 sticks plus 5 tablespoons (21 tablespoons/300 g) unsalted butter

2 tablespoons (40 g) light corn syrup

2 tablespoons plus 1 teaspoon (40 g) fine sea salt

2 tablespoons (40 g) vanilla paste

2 tablespoons plus 1 teaspoon (40 g) baking soda

1 pound (455 g) 64% dark chocolate, coarsely chopped

¼ cup (60 ml) caramel sauce

Line a 13 by 18-inch (33 by 46-cm) baking sheet with parchment paper and set a cooling rack over a second baking sheet.

In a medium saucepan, combine the sugar, butter, corn syrup, salt, vanilla paste, and ¼ cup (60 ml) water and place over medium heat. Stir until the butter is incorporated and the mixture is thin but cloudy.

Bring the mixture to a boil, then let it cook, swirling the pan occasionally, until it is amber in color and a candy thermometer registers 290°F/143°C, 10 to 15 minutes.

Remove the pan from the heat and immediately whisk in the baking soda until just incorporated. The mixture will start to foam.

Use a silicone spatula to pour the mixture onto the parchment-lined baking sheet, but do not spread the mixture with the spatula or compress it. Set aside to cool completely, at least 30 minutes.

Lift out the parchment paper and toffee. Rap it against the counter and use your fingers to break the candy into whatever size pieces you prefer.

In the top of a double boiler (or a heatproof bowl set over a pot of simmering water), warm 12 ounces (340 g) of the chocolate until it is melted and a candy thermometer registers 113°F/45°C. Remove from the heat. Add the remaining 4 ounces (115 g) chocolate and stir constantly until it is melted and the thermometer registers 90°F/32°C.

Dip the toffee pieces in the chocolate, letting the excess drip off. Place the dipped pieces on the wire rack set over a baking sheet and allow to set in a cool place or the refrigerator, about 15 minutes. The toffee will keep in an airtight container for up to 2 weeks. To serve, stack pieces of toffee and drizzle with caramel sauce.

Florentines

These cookies were either named by the courtly French chefs to honor Queen Catherine de Medici or because they resemble her native city's gold florin. When I include these cookies in a dessert buffet, I always notice guests going back for seconds. They're irresistible.

• MAKES ABOUT 32 COOKIES •

2¾ cups (200 g) sliced blanched almonds

7 tablespoons (100 g) unsalted butter, plus more for pans

½ cup (120 ml) heavy cream

½ cup (100 g) sugar

2 tablespoons plus 1 teaspoon (45 g) honey

¼ cup (50 g) dried cherries, cut into small dice

¼ cup (50 g) candied orange peel, cut into small dice, optional

¼ cup plus 3 tablespoons (55 g) all-purpose flour

8 ounces (225 g) 64% dark chocolate, chopped

Preheat the oven to 375°F/190°C (or use a toaster oven and work in batches). Spread the almonds on a baking sheet and toast, stirring once or twice, until lightly golden, about 8 minutes. Set aside to cool. Turn off the oven.

Butter a 9-inch (23-cm) square baking pan.

In a small saucepan, combine the 7 tablespoons (100 g) butter, cream, sugar, and honey and place over medium heat. Cook, stirring constantly, until the mixture is melted and comes to a boil. Boil without stirring until a candy thermometer registers 250°F/120°C, or until a small amount of the mixture dropped into a cup of ice water forms a ball, about 8 minutes. Remove from the heat.

Add the almonds, cherries, and orange peel, if using, and stir to combine. Stir in the flour until blended. Pour the mixture into the buttered pan and set aside until cool enough to handle, at least 1 hour.

Preheat the oven to 425°F/220°C. Butter 4 baking sheets. Use a spoon to scoop balls of dough of equal size and place them on the prepared pans, leaving a generous amount of space between them. With wet fingers or the back of a fork dipped in cold water, press the balls of dough as thin as possible.

Bake until the Florentines are golden, 4 to 5 minutes. Watch carefully to prevent burning. Cool on the pans on racks.

To temper the chocolate, in the top of a double boiler (or a heatproof bowl set over a pot of simmering water) warm 6 ounces (170 g) of the chocolate until it is melted and a candy thermometer registers 115°F/45°C. Remove from the heat. Add the remaining 2 ounces (55 g) chocolate and stir constantly until it is melted and the thermometer registers 90°F/32°C. Allow to cool slightly before proceeding.

Holding a cookie with your fingers, dip the flat side in the chocolate and place on a piece of parchment paper, chocolate-side up. Repeat with the remaining cookies and leave at room temperature to set, or refrigerate to speed up the process. Store in an airtight container for up to 2 weeks.

Molten Chocolate Cakes

Thick and decadent, these individual cakes use MarieBelle Aztec Hot Chocolate. If you prefer to bake a solid cake that can then be unmolded (and that does not contain raw eggs, which some people cannot consume), you can bake the batter in a buttered 8-inch (20-cm) springform pan until the center is set, about 10 to 15 minutes. Cool in the pan on a rack, then unbuckle the ring and serve.

• SERVES 6 •

1 stick plus 6 tablespoons (14 tablespoons/200 g) unsalted butter, plus more for the ramekins

2 cups plus 2 teaspoons (255 g) MarieBelle Aztec Hot Chocolate

4 large eggs

1¼ cups (145 g) confectioners' sugar, plus more for dusting

½ cup (65 g) all-purpose flour

Salted crème fraîche, for serving, optional

Preheat the oven to 325°F/165°C.

Butter six 3½-inch (9-cm) ramekins and place them on a baking sheet.

In a double boiler (or a heatproof bowl set over a pot of simmering water), warm the butter and hot chocolate, stirring occasionally, until smooth and melted.

In a large bowl, beat together the eggs, sugar, and flour with an electric mixer on medium speed until pale and thick.

Fold in the chocolate until just combined.

Divide the batter evenly among the prepared ramekins. Bake until the edges are set but the centers are still soft, 10 to 15 minutes.

Allow to cool briefly until warm and no longer hot, then sprinkle with confectioners' sugar and serve in the ramekins with salted crème fraîche, if desired.

Dimitri's Flourless Chocolate Cake

Flourless chocolate cake is dense and delicious, not to mention a treat that even friends with gluten issues can enjoy. This rustic cake is meant to crack and sink in the center. It always makes a big impression. My great friend Dimitri is HRH Dimitri of Yugoslavia.

• SERVES 8 TO 10 •

2 sticks plus 2 tablespoons (18 tablespoons/250 g) unsalted butter, cut into cubes, at room temperature, plus more for the pan

9 ounces (250 g) 72% dark chocolate, chopped

1¼ cups (250 g) granulated sugar

11 large eggs, separated

Confectioners' sugar, for sprinkling

Preheat the oven to 350°F/175°C.

Brush a 9-inch (23-cm) springform pan with butter.

In the top of a double boiler (or a heatproof bowl set over a pot of simmering water), warm the chocolate, stirring occasionally, until smooth.

Remove from the heat, add the butter, and stir until melted and combined.

In a large bowl, combine the granulated sugar with the egg yolks. Whisk until pale and thick, about 5 minutes. Add the chocolate to the egg yolk mixture and whisk until combined.

In another large bowl, beat the egg whites with an electric mixer on medium-high speed to stiff peaks, about 6 minutes. Fold the chocolate mixture into the egg whites until just combined.

Pour the batter into the prepared cake pan. Bake until the top is set and crackled, about 30 minutes. (Inserting a tester won't tell you whether the cake is done, as it remains soft in the center.)

Let the cake cool completely in the pan on a wire rack. Unbuckle and remove the ring from the pan. Dust the cake with confectioners' sugar and serve.

Marie Antoinette Ganache Cake

Marie Antoinette's sense of style is inspiring to me. This cake, an ode to her lavish lifestyle, is served in small pieces, as it is very rich. Ganache—the chocolate and cream confection shaped into truffles and used in numerous other ways in the sweet kitchen—was introduced in 1869 by Parisian confectioner Paul Siraudin. He took the name of his invention from *Les Ganaches*, a then-popular satirical comedy, which in turn inspired me to write my very own "Ode de Chocolat" (see front endpaper).

• MAKES 24 PIECES •

GANACHE

13½ ounces (380 g) 64% dark chocolate, chopped

1½ cups (360 ml) heavy cream

¼ cup (80 g) inverted sugar (see Note, page 21) or light corn syrup

3¼ ounces (90 g) hazelnut paste

2½ tablespoons (35 g) unsalted butter, at room temperature

2 tablespoons (15 g) cocoa powder

Edible gold powder, for finishing

BASE

2⅓ cups (165 g) feuilletine

5 ounces (140 g) 38% milk chocolate, chopped

5 ounces (140 g) hazelnut paste

2 teaspoons (9 g) cocoa butter

For the ganache, place the dark chocolate in a medium heatproof bowl. In a small saucepan, bring the cream and inverted sugar to a boil over medium heat. Remove from the heat and pour over the dark chocolate. Let stand for 2 minutes to melt, then stir with a silicone spatula to combine. Add the hazelnut paste to the chocolate mixture and stir to combine. Add the butter and stir until melted. Set aside.

For the base, put the feuilletine in a medium bowl and crush it further by hand. In the top of a double boiler (or a heatproof bowl set over a pot of simmering water), combine the milk chocolate, hazelnut paste, and cocoa butter. Cook, stirring, over medium heat, until melted and combined.

Remove from the heat and stir the mixture until a candy thermometer registers 100°F/38°C, 8 to 10 minutes. Stir in the feuilletine.

Line a 9 by 13-inch (23 by 33-cm) baking sheet with plastic wrap, leaving some overhanging the sides for easy unmolding. Spread the base into the pan using an offset spatula to create a smooth, even layer. Pour the ganache on top and spread it in an even layer. Cover and let the cake set at cool room temperature for 8 hours.

To serve, lift the cake out of the pan and transfer to a cutting board. Fill a tall pitcher or vase with very hot water. Warm a long sharp knife by dipping the blade in the water, then wiping it dry. Use the knife to cut the cake into 24 equal rectangular pieces (each about 4 by 1-inch/10 by 2.5-cm), warming the knife in the water and then wiping it off between each cut.

Before serving, use a pastry brush to brush the cocoa powder on the top and around the sides of each piece. Decorate the top of each with a stencil using the edible gold powder.

- IN -

HONDURAS

Millennia in the making, modern Honduran cuisine is based on the native Mesoamerican crops, including maize, tomatoes, peppers, and fish from the Pacific Ocean, the Caribbean Sea, and lakes, among them Lake Yojoa.

With the arrival of the Spanish in the sixteenth century, the Honduran diet expanded to include the meat of domesticated animals, such as beef, pork, and chicken. The beef from the Olancho region is featured in the hearty stew Tapado Olanchano (page 75), while conch from the coast is the star of Sopa de Caracol (page 55).

MARIBEL'S MENUS

(recipes in roman are provided)

A GARDEN BREAKFAST
Hacienda San Lucas, Copán

MarieBelle's Hot Chocolate ... 18
Fried Ripe Plantains ... 42
Tropical Fruit Salad ... 42
Alborotos ... 45
Sweet Corn Pancakes ... 46
Hojuelas ... 46
Mantequilla Crema

AN ISLAND LUNCH
Cayos Cochinos

Iced Mint Tea with Orange Slices & Fresh Mint
Red Cabbage & Onion Salad ... 50
Sopa de Capirotadas ... 51
Fried Corvina ... 52
Chimichurri ... 52
Sopa de Caracol ... 55

PICNIC BY THE BEACH
Cayos Cochinos

Pan de Coco ... 60
Pan Bagnat Sandwiches ... 61
Fried Ripe Plantains
Yuca Fritters with Grated Tomato Sauce & Romesco ... 62
Watermelon Slices

TROPICAL HARVEST SUPPER
Hacienda San Lucas, Copán

Chardonnay
Basmati Rice with Cilantro, Dill & Potatoes ... 68
Blended Beans My Way ... 71
Grated Tomato Sauce ... 71
Vegetarian Pupusas ... 72
Cucumber & Tomato Salad ... 72
Tapado Olanchano ... 75

---

*Opposite: Sandwiches and watermelon are the perfect accompaniment to a day spent near the beach in the Bay Islands of Honduras. **Following pages, clockwise from left:** Fresh cacao pods with dried cocoa beans; a bunch of plantains hang in the kitchen of a Milpa farm; open-fire island cooking; Maribel stands beneath a cacao tree; a characteristic boat on the beach.*

A GARDEN BREAKFAST

In Honduras, dried corn is soaked with lime and boiled or cooked in ash. This ancient Mesoamerican tradition of medicinal benefit is known as nixtamalization, and is believed to have originated 3,000 years ago. Corn is still a major part of the local diet in Honduras and is served at almost every meal in one form or another—even in chocolate-dipped Alborotos (page 45).

Opposite: As the night air slowly makes way for the tropical warmth of the rising sun, a patio shaded by a pergola is the perfect spot for an outdoor breakfast.

Fried Ripe Plantains

In the center front of the image opposite are fried plantains. Unlike bananas, green plantains cannot be eaten raw. Though technically a fruit, plantains are prepared in both sweet and savory dishes.

• SERVES 4 •

½ cup (120 ml) vegetable oil

4 tablespoons (56 g) unsalted butter

2 ripe plantains, peeled and cut lengthwise into ¼-inch- (6-mm-) thick slices

Mantequilla crema (Honduran crema) or salted crème fraîche, for serving

In a medium skillet, heat the oil and butter over medium heat.

When the oil mixture is hot, carefully add the plantains in a single layer and fry until golden brown, turning once, about 7 minutes per side. Watch carefully so they do not burn.

Remove the plantains with a slotted spatula and drain briefly on a plate lined with paper towels . Serve with mantequilla crema.

Tropical Fruit Salad

While the papaya tree was first domesticated in Mesoamerica, the mango tree originated in Southern Asia. In this tropical fruit medley, the delicate flavors of East and West are awakened by the distinctive tang of lime.

• SERVES 4 TO 6 •

2 cups (300 g) ¾-inch (2-cm) cubes watermelon

1 cup (165 g) ½-inch (1.25-cm) cubes pineapple

1 mango, peeled, pitted, and cut into ¾-inch (2-cm) dice

1 papaya, peeled, pitted, and cut into ¾-inch (2-cm) dice

½ cup (120 ml) freshly squeezed orange juice

¼ cup (80 g) honey or pure maple syrup

Leaves of 2 sprigs fresh mint, torn if large

1 teaspoon (4 g) grated lime zest

2 tablespoons (30 ml) freshly squeezed lime juice

¼ cup (22 g) unsweetened coconut flakes or shredded coconut, toasted, optional

Combine the watermelon, pineapple, mango, and papaya in a large bowl. Whisk together the orange juice, honey, mint, and lime zest and juice in a small bowl.

 Pour the dressing over the fruit and toss to combine well. Sprinkle with coconut before serving, if desired.

Alborotos

In the top center of the image opposite, near the tropical fruit salad, the two small bowls each contain a chocolate-dipped corn ball known as an alboroto. Like all six types of corn, popcorn originates from a wild grass. However, despite it closely resembling corn-on-the-cob, only popcorn kernels have the ability to pop.

• MAKES 8 TO 10 BALLS, ABOUT 4 SERVINGS •

1 cup (200 g) granulated or turbinado sugar

½ cup (120 ml) light corn syrup

4 cups (32 g) air-popped plain popcorn

Vegetable oil, for coating hands

10 ounces (280 g) 64% dark chocolate, coarsely chopped

In a small saucepan, combine the sugar, corn syrup, and ½ cup (120 ml) water over medium heat. Stir until the sugar is dissolved. Bring to a boil, then cook, swirling the pan occasionally, until the mixture is caramel in color and a candy thermometer registers 245°F/120°C, about 20 minutes. Set aside to rest off the heat until cool enough to touch, about 15 minutes.

Place the popcorn in a large bowl and pour the caramel over it. Using a spoon, mix until the popcorn is evenly coated.

Immediately coat your hands with some oil to prevent the caramel from sticking and form the mixture into 2½-inch (6.5-cm) balls (about the size of tennis balls).

Allow the alborotos to cool completely on a parchment-lined baking sheet.

To temper the chocolate, warm 7 ounces (200 g) of the chocolate in the top of a double boiler (or a heatproof bowl set over a pot of simmering water) until it is melted and a candy thermometer registers 113°F/45°C. Remove from the heat. Add the remaining 3 ounces (80 g) chocolate and stir constantly until it is melted and the thermometer registers 89.6°F/32°C.

Dip the alborotos halfway in the chocolate, letting the excess drip off. Return to the baking sheet and allow to set in a cool place, about 15 minutes.

Sweet Corn Pancakes

On the lower left of the image opposite is a plate of sweet corn pancakes. Sweet corn is widely cultivated and is the extra-sweet variety of the maize species. Serve these pancakes with a dollop of salted crème fraîche (or mantequilla crema), seen in the terrine.

• MAKES 8 PANCAKES •

2 ears sweet corn, kernels cut off, or one 11-ounce (33-g) can sweet corn, drained

2 tablespoons (30 g) unsalted butter, melted

2 large eggs

²⁄₃ cup (80 g) self-rising flour

1 tablespoon (12 g) sugar

Pinch kosher salt

2 scallions, finely chopped

¼ cup (60 ml) vegetable oil

In a blender, puree the corn until smooth.

In a medium bowl, whisk together the butter and eggs. Add the flour, sugar, salt, and scallions and mix to combine. Mix in the corn.

In a medium skillet, heat the oil over medium heat. When the oil is hot, drop in large spoonfuls of the batter, making sure not to crowd the pan, and fry, turning once, until the pancakes are puffed and golden, 1 to 2 minutes per side. Transfer the pancakes to a plate lined with paper towels to drain briefly. Repeat with the remaining batter and serve hot.

Hojuelas

Hojuelas are typical Honduran fritters made at home and also sold in street stalls. They shine when topped with a drizzle of dark chocolate.

• MAKES 10 FRITTERS •

1 large egg

1 teaspoon (4 g) sugar

Pinch kosher salt

2 tablespoons (30 ml) milk

1 tablespoon (15 g) unsalted butter, melted

1 cup (125 g) all-purpose flour, sifted, plus more for dusting

Vegetable oil, for brushing and frying

4 ounces (115 g) 64% dark chocolate, coarsely chopped

In a medium bowl, whisk together the egg, sugar, and salt. Add the milk and butter and stir to combine well.

Gradually mix in the sifted flour. Knead the dough by hand until it is smooth and well-combined and doesn't stick to your hands, about 5 minutes. Shape the dough into 10 equal-size balls. Brush them with oil and let rest on a baking sheet for 30 minutes.

On a floured work surface, roll out each ball as thinly as possible into a disk, occasionally lifting and rotating it so it doesn't stick to the surface.

Fill a large deep skillet or Dutch oven with 2 inches (5 cm) oil and place over medium-high heat. When the oil is hot, 350°F/175°C, carefully slip a disk of dough into the skillet and fry until golden, about 2 minutes. Turn and cook until golden on the second side, about 1 additional minute. Transfer to a plate lined with paper towels to drain. Repeat with the remaining disks.

Warm the chocolate in the top of a double boiler (or a heatproof bowl set over a pot of simmering water), stirring occasionally, until smooth. Drizzle the chocolate over the hojuelas before serving.

AN ISLAND LUNCH

In the early sixteenth century, on his fourth voyage to the continent, Christopher Columbus became the first European to set foot on Guanaja, one of the Bay Islands in the Gulf of Honduras. Soon after he returned to Spain, others arrived—European settlers, traders, and even pirates made their home in these islands. In 1859 they definitively became part of Honduras.

Opposite: Hondurans have long considered their seashore a place suitable for farming. Among the crops cultivated there is the coconut. The year-round tropical weather also makes the Honduran coastlines on the Caribbean Sea and the Pacific Ocean beautifully suited for outdoor dining.

Red Cabbage & Onion Salad

Red onions, with their distinct spicy yet mild flavor, are a perfect salad mixer. The cabbage and onion combination achieves a complexity greater than the sum of its parts.

• SERVES 6 TO 8 •

¼ cup (120 ml) distilled white vinegar

¼ teaspoon (1 g) ground cumin

Juice of 1 lime

Kosher salt and freshly ground black pepper

1 medium red onion, diced

1 jalapeño pepper, minced

½ head red cabbage, cored and finely shredded

1 pint (8 ounces/225 g) cherry tomatoes on the vine

½ cup (20 g) fresh cilantro leaves, finely chopped, plus whole leaves for garnish

To make the dressing, in a small bowl, whisk together the vinegar, cumin, and lime juice. Season with salt and pepper.

In a large bowl, combine the onion, jalapeño, cabbage, and dressing and toss to coat. Cover and refrigerate for about 2 hours. Top with the tomatoes and garnish with the cilantro leaves before serving.

Sopa de Capirotadas
Cheese & Corn Dumpling Soup

There are many variations of sopa de capirotadas, a popular cheese dumpling soup traditionally made with queso seco, a Central American cheese. Queso seco is dry, hard, and salty and crumbles easily, which allows the dumplings to hold together when immersed in the liquid. Adding the dumplings right before serving preserves their crunchy texture.

• SERVES 8 •

1 cup plus 1 tablespoon (135 g) masa harina

1 cup (240 g) Honduran queso fresco, cotija, or Parmigiano Reggiano, crumbled or grated

1 cup (240 g) shredded mozzarella

2 large eggs, lightly beaten

Kosher salt and freshly ground black pepper

Vegetable oil, for frying

1 quart (1 l) vegetable or beef broth

Leaves of 1 small bunch cilantro, chopped

In a large bowl, combine 1 cup (125 g) masa harina, the queso fresco, mozzarella, eggs, and salt and pepper. Mix to incorporate, then gradually add 2 cups (480 ml) water while kneading with your hands until a smooth dough forms.

Use a soup spoon to scoop balls of dough, then gently flatten them with your palms to form small round patties, about 2 inches (5 cm) wide and ½ inch (1.2 cm) thick, making 8 dumplings.

Fill a large deep skillet or large Dutch oven with about 2 inches (5 cm) oil. When the oil is hot, carefully add some dumplings, making sure not to crowd the pan, and cook, turning once, until golden brown, 4 to 6 minutes per side.

Transfer the dumplings to a plate lined with paper towels. Repeat with the remaining patties.

Warm the broth in a medium saucepan over medium heat. Combine the remaining 1 tablespoon (10 g) masa harina with 2 tablespoons (30 ml) water in a small bowl and stir to combine. Stir the mixture into the broth and add salt and pepper to taste. Simmer for 5 minutes, then add the cilantro.

Ladle the broth into individual serving bowls and add dumplings to each.

Fried Corvina

Like Atlantic striped or black sea bass and Mediterranean branzino, Caribbean corvina is a sea bass with a mild, sweet taste and firm, large-flaked flesh. Serve with a traditional chimichurri sauce and a red onion and cabbage salad.

• SERVES 4 •

4 whole corvina or branzino (14 oz to 1 lb/400 to 455 g each), cleaned

¼ cup (60 ml) extra-virgin olive oil, plus more if necessary

4 cloves garlic, finely chopped

½ large white onion, finely chopped

1 tablespoon (3 g) dried oregano

Kosher salt and freshly ground black pepper

Vegetable oil, for frying

Cilantro leaves and sliced jalapeño peppers, for garnish

Lemon wedges, for serving

Rinse the fish well and pat dry with paper towels. Cut 3 deep slits on both sides of each fish with a sharp knife. Place the fish in a large bowl or baking dish. Top the fish with the olive oil, garlic, onion, oregano, and some salt and pepper and massage into the fish. Cover and refrigerate for at least 4 hours and up to 1 day.

When ready to cook, pat the fish dry with paper towels and let sit for 1 hour to come to room temperature.

Fill a large nonstick skillet with 1½ inches (3.8 cm) vegetable oil and heat over medium-high heat. When the oil is hot, carefully add one fish and cook until golden brown, gently lifting the edge of the fish with a spatula to check the color, about 5 minutes. Carefully turn the fish and let the second side cook, basting with oil on top a couple of times, until golden brown, about 5 minutes. The total frying time should be no longer than 15 minutes.

Transfer to a baking sheet lined with parchment paper and keep in a low oven to stay warm. Repeat with the remaining fish, adding more oil as needed. Remove the fish from the oven and sprinkle each one with cilantro and jalapeño. Serve with lemon wedges.

Chimichurri

On this quiet Cayos beach, Caribbean corvina is served with a traditional chimichurri sauce. The jalapeño peppers used in the sauce are milder in heat than cayenne peppers, the perfect counterbalance to the refined and mild flavor of the fish.

• MAKES 2 CUPS •

¼ cup (60 ml) red wine vinegar

4 cloves garlic, finely chopped

1 shallot, finely chopped

1 jalapeño pepper, finely chopped

2 cups (80 g) cilantro leaves, finely chopped

2 cups (80 g) flat-leaf parsley leaves, finely chopped

1 cup (240 ml) extra-virgin olive oil

3 tablespoons (21 g) finely ground almonds, optional

Kosher salt

In a medium bowl, combine the vinegar, garlic, shallot, and jalapeño. Mix well and let sit at room temperature for about 1 hour.

Add the cilantro, parsley, oil, and almonds, if using. Salt to taste. Mix well to combine. Cover and refrigerate until ready to serve.

Sopa de Caracol
Conch Chowder

Coconuts, limes, and tomatoes are laid out on a table made from a local fishing boat, in preparation for an evening meal of sopa de caracol, or conch chowder. This traditional Honduran dish is popular throughout the Florida Keys, as well as on many Caribbean islands. Sometimes other locally caught fish and shellfish besides conch are added.

• SERVES 8 •

2 quarts (2 l) chicken broth

3 cloves garlic, finely chopped

2 large white onions, finely chopped

2 jalapeño peppers, seeded and thinly sliced

1 green bell pepper, seeded and thinly sliced

One 1-inch (2.5-cm) piece ginger, smashed

3 green bananas, cut into ¼- inch (6.5-mm) slices

3 carrots, cut into ¼-inch (6.5-mm) slices

2 pounds (910 g) yuca, peeled and cut in ¼-inch (6.5-mm) slices

Two 14-ounce (420-ml) cans unsweetened coconut milk

2 tablespoons (30 ml) fish sauce

Kosher salt and freshly ground black pepper

Pinch ground annatto, optional

2 pounds (910 g) conch meat, cleaned and diced

1 pound (455 g) firm white fish, such as swordfish, mahi mahi, or cod, cut into 4 pieces

1 pound (455 g) shrimp, peeled and deveined

Leaves of ½ bunch cilantro, finely chopped

Lime wedges, for serving, optional

In a large stockpot or Dutch oven, combine the chicken broth, garlic, onions, jalapeño, bell pepper, and ginger over medium-high heat and bring to a simmer. Add the green bananas, carrots, and yuca. Cover the pot and simmer until the vegetables are tender, 15 to 20 minutes.

Add the coconut milk, fish sauce, and salt and pepper to taste. Add the annatto, if desired. (It turns the chowder a bright orange color.) Cook for 10 minutes more to meld the flavors. Remove and discard the ginger.

Add the conch and cook until tender, about 10 minutes. Add the fish and shrimp and cook until the fish is opaque and the shrimp are pink, 3 to 5 minutes. Remove from the heat and add the cilantro. Serve with lime wedges, if desired.

A Never-Ending Journey

The Lenca people have no written language, so the history of the Lenca civilization has been passed down through the generations with oral stories recounted at family gatherings and shared by travelers through the centuries.

Tim Lohrentz, who blogs at *The Indigenous History of El Salvador*, explains that Conchagua (a place near the border between Guatemala and Honduras) has several meanings, one of which is a reference to two parts, or a duality, which may indicate that in Conchagua the Olmecs and Lenca separated and became two distinct societies.

Lohrentz recounts an oft-repeated Lenca myth that Maribel recalled from her own childhood. When the Olmecs and Lenca were still one people, it is said part of their kingdom slipped into the sea. They sent out a large expedition to locate this lost land. Ixo-Kelkele, his wife Ulul, and Chief Aranuka, as well as priests, servants, artisans, doctors, magicians, dancers, navigators, and experts in reading the stars, all sailed into the ocean.

They placed guiding lights inside bowls and set them afloat on the water to show them the way. However, the expedition never returned and the Olmecs settled in a new home on the Pacific coast.

Opposite: The conch is not just a beautiful seashell and an important source of food; it is also a symbol of the ancient Aztec culture, whose people used the shell as a horn or trumpet. It is said that the conch was the instrument that Quetzalcoatl played to defeat the challenge of the Lord of the Dead.

PICNIC BY THE BEACH

Modern-day inhabitants of the Cayos Cochinos islands in the Bay of Honduras trace their ancestry to the Caribs, who were deported by the British from Saint Vincent after they seized the island from the French in the eighteenth century. These islands are relatively far from the mainland, and that distance has kept local beliefs and traditions alive. Their sandy beaches are the perfect spot for a picnic.

Opposite: Two young girls from the local fishing community enjoy Pan Bagnat Sandwiches (page 61) on locally baked buns.

Pan de Coco

Pan de coco originated in Honduras, then the recipe was brought to the Philippines by the Spanish during the colonial era, and soon it became a staple of Filipino cuisine as well. On the Cayos, the bread is cooked in an ingenious traditional wood-fired stove and oven.

• MAKES 8 BUNS •

2 cups (250 g) all-purpose flour, plus more for dusting

2/3 cup (150 g) coconut milk

3 tablespoons (25 g) coconut flour

1 teaspoon (4 g) sugar

1/2 teaspoon (2 g) kosher salt

1/2 teaspoon (2 ml) coconut oil, plus more for brushing

1¼ teaspoons (3.5 g) active dry yeast

In a large bowl, combine the all-purpose flour, coconut milk, coconut flour, sugar, salt, 1/2 teaspoon (2 ml) coconut oil, and yeast. Knead until smooth and elastic, about 10 minutes.

Oil a large bowl. Add the dough, cover with a clean kitchen towel, and let rise until doubled in size, about 1 hour.

Preheat the oven to 375°F/190°C.

On a floured work surface, divide the dough into 8 equal pieces and form into balls (about the size of tennis balls). Transfer to a parchment-lined baking sheet, spacing the balls evenly with plenty of room to rise.

Brush the balls with coconut oil, cover, and let them rise until doubled in size and they are just touching one another, 30 to 45 minutes. Bake, uncovered, until golden, 25 to 30 minutes. Cool slightly.

Pan Bagnat Sandwiches

Pan bagnat sandwiches on pan de coco make a light picnic lunch. Pan bagnat, sometimes spelled pain bagnat, my favorite picnic sandwich, originated in the area near Nice in France. The name translates as wet sandwich. The crucial ingredients are good-quality canned tuna and ripe tomatoes. The oil of the tuna and the juice of the tomato "wet" the bread.

• SERVES 6 •

Kosher salt

1 pound (455 g) yellow wax beans, trimmed

6 Pan de Coco (recipe opposite), pan bagnat rolls or, brioche buns

Extra-virgin olive oil, for drizzling

1 tablespoon (15 g) roasted garlic paste

1 tablespoon (15 g) olive tapenade

12 ounces (340 g) good-quality tuna packed in olive oil, drained well

4 ripe plum tomatoes, sliced

2 piquillo peppers, each cut lengthwise into 6 strips, optional

½ medium red onion, thinly sliced

Freshly ground black pepper

4 hard-boiled eggs, peeled and sliced

12 basil leaves

Preheat the broiler.

Bring a large saucepan of water to a boil. Salt generously, then add the beans and cook until crisp-tender, about 5 minutes. Drain and reserve.

Halve the bread lengthwise and pull out some of the crumb from the middle of each piece to make a well. (Reserve for breadcrumbs or another use.) Arrange the bread on a baking sheet, cut sides up. Drizzle with olive oil and broil until golden, 1 to 2 minutes.

Spread the top pieces of bread with garlic paste and the bottom pieces with the olive tapenade. On the bottom pieces, layer the tuna, beans, tomato, piquillo peppers (if using), and onion. Drizzle with olive oil and season with salt and pepper. Add egg slices and basil.

Put the sandwich tops on the bottoms and press down on each to flatten and meld the flavors. Wrap tightly with plastic wrap and refrigerate for 1 hour before serving.

Yuca Fritters
with Grated Tomato Sauce & Romesco

Both plantain and yuca fritters are staples of Latin American cuisine. Yuca, or cassava, is a root that has a rough, bark-like skin that must be scraped off before cooking. Whether served as a snack, vegetable accompaniment, or an appetizer, yuca fritters are always a winner. I like to top them with either a grated tomato sauce or romesco.

• SERVES 6 •

1 tablespoon (15 g) kosher salt, plus more to taste

1 pound (455 g) yuca, peeled and diced

¼ cup (60 ml) extra-virgin olive oil

1 tablespoon (15 g) roasted garlic paste

1 large egg, beaten

Leaves of ½ bunch cilantro, chopped

1 cup (240 ml) vegetable oil

3 tablespoons (30 g) whole blanched almonds, toasted, as garnish, optional

Romesco, recipe follows, for serving

Grated Tomato Sauce (see page 71), for serving

Bring a medium saucepan of water to a boil. Add 1 tablespoon (15 g) salt, then add the yuca and cook until it is tender enough to mash, 15 to 30 minutes.

Drain, transfer to a medium bowl, and mash until almost perfectly smooth (little chunks are okay). When you squeeze a bit of the mixture in your hand it should form a ball.

Add the olive oil, garlic paste, egg, and cilantro and mix until well combined. Season to taste with salt.

With a soup spoon, pull off a small amount of the mixture. Shape into a ball, then gently flatten into a patty about ½ inch (12 mm) thick and 2 inches (5 cm) in diameter. Repeat with the remaining mixture, making about 12 fritters.

Heat the vegetable oil in a large skillet over medium-high heat. When the oil is hot, carefully add some patties, making sure not to crowd the pan, and cook until golden brown, 3 to 5 minutes per side.

Transfer the fritters to a plate lined with paper towels. Repeat with the remaining patties. Garnish with the almonds (if using). Serve with the sauces.

Romesco

Reddish-orange romesco is both sweet and rich. A sauce that originated in Catalonia, Spain, it is traditionally served with fish or seafood but is also a delicious dipping sauce for fritters.

• MAKES 2 CUPS (950 G) •

One 12-ounce (340g) jar roasted red peppers, drained

One 14.5-ounce (411g) can fire-roasted tomatoes, drained

¾ cup (110 g) blanched almonds, toasted

¼ cup (32 g) pistachios, toasted

¼ cup (60 ml) extra-virgin olive oil

2 cloves garlic, crushed and peeled

Juice of ½ lemon

1 teaspoon (5 ml) Champagne vinegar

1 teaspoon (5 g) kosher salt, plus more to taste

Combine the peppers, tomatoes, almonds, pistachios, olive oil, garlic, lemon juice, vinegar, and 1 teaspoon (5 g) salt in a food processor fitted with the metal blade. Process until almost smooth (a bit of texture is okay), scraping down the sides of the work bowl as needed. Taste and season with more salt, if needed.

Transfer to a serving bowl.

Above, left to right: Cutting cacao pods; Stela N South depicting the fifteenth ruler of Copán; refreshing watermelon slices; lobster traps on Cayos Cochinos.

TROPICAL HARVEST SUPPER

Honduras is home to more than 5,000 different plant species that grow in its jungles, dry conifer forests, coral reefs, and mangroves. Native Mesoamerican cultivars include avocados and corn. The Mayans cultivated tomatoes long before Cortés encountered them in 1519 and brought them back to Europe. Honduras also grows a wide variety of hibiscus flowers.

Opposite: A centerpiece of red hibiscus flowers brightens a table surrounded by lush plant life. Botanist Carl Linnaeus collected a Honduran specimen of the Hibiscus rosa-sinensis, *giving it this name in 1753.*

Basmati Rice
with Cilantro, Dill & Potatoes

This dish showcases the subtle flavor of basmati rice. Basmati rice has very long, slim grains and is grown in northern India and Pakistan. Rice grown elsewhere cannot be labeled as basmati.

• SERVES 6 TO 8 •

2 cups (370 g) basmati rice, rinsed

1 teaspoon (5 g) kosher salt, plus more to taste

Leaves of ½ bunch cilantro, finely chopped

Fronds of ½ bunch dill, finely chopped, or 1 tablespoon (3 g) dried dill

2 russet potatoes, peeled and very thinly sliced

1 stick (8 tablespoons/113 g) unsalted butter, melted

Olive oil, for brushing

Fill a large (preferably nonstick) pot with a tight-fitting lid with 3 quarts (3 l) water and bring to a boil. Add the rice and 1 teaspoon (5 g) salt and boil until al dente, about 10 minutes. Drain and transfer the rice to a medium bowl. (Reserve the pot.) Add the cilantro and dill to the rice and gently toss to combine; taste and adjust salt if necessary.

In a medium bowl, combine the potatoes and butter, season with salt, and toss to coat. Brush the bottom and sides of the reserved pot with olive oil. Line the bottom and sides with the potatoes in a single layer. Pour any leftover butter from the bowl into the bottom of the pot.

Carefully spoon the rice into the pot, doing your best not to disturb the potatoes. Use the handle of a wooden spoon to poke 6 holes in the rice. Place a clean kitchen towel or heavy-duty paper towel between the top of the pot and the lid. This will help the rice steam.

Return the pot to medium-low heat and cook until the rice is tender and the potatoes are browned and crispy. This will likely take about 25 minutes, but you can start checking after 18 minutes.

Serve immediately in a large shallow bowl. Be sure each guest gets some of the potato crust, which will mix with the rice as you begin to serve.

Blended Beans My Way

Red beans, which are similar in color to kidney beans but smaller in size, are frequently used in Honduran cuisine. They are a common sight on kitchen tables—no Honduran pantry is complete without them.

• SERVES 6 TO 8 •

2 cups (455 g) dried red beans, rinsed

1 tablespoon (15 g) kosher salt, plus more to taste

Freshly ground black pepper

¼ bunch cilantro sprigs

1 large Spanish onion, quartered

1 green bell pepper, seeded and quartered

1 large tomato, quartered

½ jalapeño pepper, seeded and cut into 4 pieces

¼ cup (60 ml) extra-virgin olive oil

Fill a large pot halfway with water. Add the beans and bring to a boil. Cover and cook on medium heat until the beans are soft and the liquid is reduced, about 1 hour. Add 1 tablespoon (15 g) salt and cook 10 additional minutes.

Allow the beans to cool. Working in batches if necessary, add the beans to a blender with their broth. Puree until smooth. The mixture will be thin. Set the beans aside in a bowl or large measuring cup.

Add the cilantro, onion, bell pepper, tomato, and jalapeño to the blender and pulse to form a paste.

In a large skillet, heat the oil over medium heat. Add the vegetable mixture and cook, stirring occasionally, until softened, about 10 minutes. Stir in the beans and add salt to taste. Cook, stirring constantly to prevent the beans from sticking, until reduced and thickened, 10 to 15 minutes.

Grated Tomato Sauce

Raw tomato sauce is quick to prepare, and grating the tomatoes delivers juicy pulp with the ideal consistency.

• MAKES ABOUT 1 CUP •

1 large ripe beefsteak tomato

3 tablespoons (45 ml) extra-virgin olive oil

1 clove garlic, finely chopped

Kosher salt and freshly ground black pepper

2 basil leaves, cut into chiffonade, optional

Trim the bottom of the tomato with a sharp knife.

Hold a box grater over a medium bowl and grate the cut side of the tomato on the largest holes until you reach the skin and stem. Discard skin and stem. To the tomato pulp add the oil and garlic, and season with salt and pepper. Sprinkle with the basil just before serving, if desired.

Vegetarian Pupusas

Pupusas, traditional corn and rice pancakes, are similar to Colombian and Venezuelan arepas. Pupusas are endlessly versatile and can be used as anything from a midday snack to the basis for a hearty dinner. Here, they are topped with a raw tomato sauce.

• SERVES 4 •

¼ cup plus 2 tablespoons (90 ml) extra-virgin olive oil

2 leeks, thinly sliced

1½ cups (185 g) masa harina

½ cup (75 g) rice flour

2 tablespoons (30 g) roasted garlic paste

Kosher salt

½ cup (120 ml) vegetable oil

Grated Tomato Sauce (see page 71), for serving

In a medium skillet, heat ¼ cup (60 ml) of the olive oil over medium heat. Add the leeks, stir to coat, reduce the heat to low, and cook, covered, stirring occasionally, until caramelized, 15 to 20 minutes.

In a large bowl, combine the masa harina and rice flour. Gradually stir in 1½ cups (360 ml) water until a loose dough forms, then knead by hand until the dough is smooth. Add the garlic paste, about half of the leeks, the remaining 2 tablespoons (30 ml) olive oil, and some salt. Continue kneading by hand until smooth.

To form a pupusa, pull off a piece of dough about the size of a golf ball and shape into a ball 1¾ inches (4.5 cm) in diameter. Use a tortilla press to press the ball into a thin disk. (Alternatively, place a ball on a piece of plastic wrap, place another piece of plastic wrap on top, and press with the bottom of a pan—a glass pie pan works well because you can see your progress—or roll with a rolling pin into a 3½-inch [9-cm] disk.) Put a small amount of the remaining leek mixture in the center of the dough, pull up the sides, and pinch them together to seal them, retaining a round shape as best as possible. Press the filled pupusa into a ¼-inch- (6-mm-) thick disk. Repeat with the remaining dough and leek mixture.

In a large skillet, heat the vegetable oil over medium-high heat. When the oil is hot, carefully add some patties, being careful not to crowd the pan, and cook until golden brown underneath, 3 to 5 minutes. Flip the patties and cook until golden on the other side, about 2 additional minutes. Transfer to a plate lined with paper towels to drain and repeat with the remaining pupusas. Serve with tomato sauce.

Cucumber & Tomato Salad

On page 74, served on a rustic table in a charming patio surrounded by abundant tropical greenery, this refreshing cucumber and tomato salad complements the traditional tapado.

• SERVES 6 •

2 kirby cucumbers, peeled, sliced, and seeded

2 medium ripe tomatoes, cut into wedges

½ medium red onion, very thinly sliced

1 cup (170 g) pitted Kalamata olives, optional

3 tablespoons (45 ml) extra-virgin olive oil

1 teaspoon fresh oregano leaves

Kosher salt and freshly ground black pepper

4 ounces (115 g) Honduran queso fresco or feta, cut into cubes, optional

6 fresh basil leaves

In a medium bowl, combine the cucumbers, tomatoes, onion, and olives, if using. Drizzle with the olive oil and sprinkle with the oregano. Season with salt and pepper to taste and toss to combine. Top with the cheese, if desired, and garnish with basil.

Tapado Olanchano
Honduran Beef Stew

Tapado Olanchano beef stew gets its name from the department of Olancho, a part of Honduras famous for cattle ranching. However, cattle are not native to the Central American country; they were brought over by the Spaniards in the sixteenth century. This Honduran classic is made with beef, pork ribs, sausages, and root vegetables. Ask your butcher to cut the pork ribs to the correct size for you.

• SERVES 6 TO 8 •

3½ pounds (1.5 kg) beef stew meat, cut into 3-inch (7.5-cm) cubes

1 quart (1 l) chicken broth

1 quart (1 l) beef broth

3½ pounds (1.5 kg) pork ribs, cut into 2½-inch (6-cm) pieces

1 tablespoon (15 g) vegetable shortening

2¼ pounds (1 kg) cured chorizo, diced

3 cloves garlic, cut into small dice

2 green bell peppers, cut into small dice

2 large tomatoes, cut into small dice

1 large yellow or white onion, cut into small dice

3 ripe plantains (peels on)

2¼ pounds (1 kg) yuca, peeled and cut into 2-inch (5-cm) pieces

2¼ pounds (1 kg) pork chicharrones, cut into 2-inch (5-cm) pieces

5 green bananas, each cut into 4 pieces

5 culantro leaves, chopped

½ cup (20 g) chopped cilantro, plus more for garnish

1 tablespoon (15 g) dried Italian seasoning

1 teaspoon (5 g) ground annatto

Kosher salt and freshly ground black pepper

In a large pot, combine the beef and chicken and beef broths. If necessary, add enough water to cover the beef. Cook over medium heat until the beef is tender, about 40 minutes. Add the pork ribs to the pot and continue to cook until the pork is tender, about 30 additional minutes. Remove the meat from the pot and place in a colander to drain. Reserve the cooking liquid.

In a medium skillet, melt the shortening over high heat. Add the chorizo and cook, stirring occasionally, until golden brown, about 5 minutes. Transfer the chorizo to a plate.

Add the garlic, bell peppers, tomatoes, and onion to the drippings in the skillet and cook over medium-low heat, stirring occasionally, until softened and fragrant, about 5 minutes. Remove from the heat.

Peel the plantains; reserve the peels and slice each plantain into 4 pieces.

In a large soup pot, arrange some of the plantain peels on the bottom in a single layer. Add the yuca, arranging it in an even layer; then add layers of the beef and pork, chorizo, chicharrones, green bananas, culantro, and cilantro. Cover the top with a layer of the remaining plantain peels.

Add the Italian seasoning and annatto to the reserved beef cooking liquid and stir to combine. Then pour the liquid down the side of the soup pot to avoid dislodging the layers. Cover the pot and cook over medium heat until the yuca and green bananas are tender and cooked through, about 20 minutes. To serve, remove the plantain peels, taste and adjust seasoning, and ladle into bowls. Garnish with cilantro.

- IN -

AMERICA

New York is a sprawling city famous for its many qualities: entrepreneurship, individualism, and perhaps most of all, its mix of cultures. Generations of cooks from all over the world have redefined and reimagined the culinary landscape of New York; their kitchens have become home to a melting pot of wonderful flavors.

New York is also the place where Maribel has made her home—drawn to live in a place infused with imported culinary traditions, the creative frontier of American cuisine.

MARIBEL'S MENUS

(recipes in roman are provided)

NEW YORK SUNDAY BRUNCH
SoHo, New York City

Fresh Orange Juice · Coffee or Tea
Smoked Salmon, Capers, Shallots & Toast · Yogurt with Honey
Crêpes Suzette . . . 84 · *Soft-boiled Eggs · Applesauce*
Sautéed Cherry Tomatoes
Blueberries, Raspberries & Strawberries
Candied Ginger

A LOFTY MEAL
SoHo, New York City

Prosecco
Sautéed Seabass with Spinach & Sauce Verte . . . 88
Sautéed Cherry Tomatoes . . . 88 · *Cipollini Onions*
MarieBelle Chocolates · Tea

LUNCH ON A TERRACE
Upper East Side, New York City

Cabernet Franc
Pork Loin Stuffed with Prunes, Walnuts & Bacon . . . 92
Roasted Root Vegetables . . . 95
Baguette with Melted Chocolate & Fresh Lavender Butter . . . 95

DINING IN LOCUST VALLEY
Locust Valley, New York

Riesling and Pinot Noir
Salmon Tartare with Cilantro . . . 100
Tiradito with Chiles & Citrus Dressing . . . 100 · Roasted Duck Breast . . . 103
Beet Puree . . . 104 · Crèpes Suzette served with crème fraîche . . . 84
MarieBelle Chocolates, Marie Antoinette Ganache Cake, Dark Chocolate Truffles
Coffee or Tea

A WHITE SATIN EVENING
SoHo, New York City

Cucumber & Tequila Cocktail . . . 110 · Skinny Margarita . . . 110 · Grapefruit Cocktail . . . 228
Roero Arneis and Bordeaux · Baguette
Citrus-Infused Fish Fillet with Grilled Tomatillos & Arugula Sprouts . . . 113
Seared Filet Mignon with Roasted Maitake Mushrooms & Fennel . . . 114
Roasted Sweet Potato Chips . . . 115

Opposite: In this SoHo loft, an Ann Ray photograph of the female form as transformed by Alexander McQueen and old-world decor are equally sensuous. Following pages, clockwise from left: Downtown Manhattan skyline; Maribel entertains; signature MarieBelle ganache chocolates celebrate New York City; the Statue of Liberty at sunset; MarieBelle's SoHo shop.

MarieBelle
NEW YORK

NEW YORK
SUNDAY BRUNCH

The midmorning meal combining savory and sweet dishes traditionally associated with breakfast and lunch, known as brunch, was imported from the UK to America. In fact, Sunday brunch has become a quintessentially New York City social gathering, giving New Yorkers an opportunity to sit down, catch up, and recharge for the week ahead.

Opposite: *Brunch is a great choice for entertaining, as most traditional brunch dishes are easy to prepare yet sophisticated. Soft-boiled eggs in classic egg cups pair with Sautéed Cherry Tomatoes (page 88), along with Crêpes Suzettes (page 84), on a beautifully set table.*

Crêpes Suzette

No one is certain of the origin of crêpes Suzette. Was it an 1895 culinary mishap served to the soon-to-be King Edward VII, as claimed by Henri Charpentier? Or was it named after the crêpes served on stage in 1897 by the popular French actress Suzanne Reichenberg, who was known as Suzette? No matter how it all began, crêpes Suzette has become a beloved classic and a brunch favorite. For a tasty variation, serve it with crème fraîche (see image on page 105).

• SERVES 6 •

BATTER

1 cup (125 g) all-purpose flour

2 cups (480 ml) whole milk

4 large eggs

4 tablespoons (57 g) unsalted butter, melted, plus more for brushing pan

1 tablespoon (12 g) sugar

Pinch kosher salt

SAUCE

Finely grated zest and juice of 1 medium orange

¼ cup plus 1 tablespoon (62 g) sugar

1 teaspoon lemon juice

4 tablespoons (57 g) unsalted butter, cut into cubes

¼ cup (60 ml) Cointreau or curaçao

¼ cup (60 ml) Benedictine or Grand Marnier

Crème fraîche for serving, optional

For the crêpes, in a medium bowl, whisk the flour, milk, and eggs until smooth with no lumps. Whisk in the 4 tablespoons melted butter, sugar, and salt.

Heat an 8- to 10-inch nonstick skillet over medium heat and brush with melted butter. Ladle in about ⅓ cup (80 ml) batter and swirl to coat the bottom of the pan. Cook until bubbles start to appear, about 1 minute. Carefully flip and cook until golden underneath, about 1 additional minute. Transfer to a plate. Brush the skillet with more butter and repeat with the remaining batter to make 12 crêpes, stacking the crêpes on the plate as they are done.

For the sauce, combine the orange zest and juice, the sugar, and the lemon juice in a large skillet over medium heat. Scatter in the butter pieces and cook, stirring, until the butter melts and the juices are bubbling. Stir well to combine. Add the liqueurs and bring to a rolling boil. Boil until thickened slightly, 1 to 2 minutes. Reduce heat to low. Fold the crêpes into quarters and slide them into the sauce, turning to coat both sides. Remove from the heat and serve immediately with their sauce. Serve with a bowl of crème fraîche, if desired.

A LOFTY MEAL

The iconic nineteenth-century cast-iron buildings in SoHo that were used for manufacturing and warehousing had mostly been abandoned by the early 1960s, when artists began moving into their empty lofts. They are credited with making SoHo into one of New York's most lively and popular areas, known for galleries and boutiques—including the flagship MarieBelle store.

This page: The polka dot ceramics are by Maria Robledo and the white ceramics are by John Born. Opposite: Displayed on a table, set near the large windows intended to provide manufacturing facilities with light, are a whimsical candlestick in the shape of a rabbit by Robin Whitman and a free-form vase by artist Anna Parsons. The wine glasses are from the Czech Republic.

Sautéed Sea Bass
with Spinach & Sauce Verte

Cool-weather spinach adds sophistication and complexity to this seafood dish, and the warm-weather tomatoes in the accompanying side dish bring bright acidity. The result is a celebration of all the growing seasons.

• SERVES 4 •

SAUCE

4 cloves garlic, crushed and peeled

4 oil-packed anchovy fillets, chopped

¼ cup (60 g) Dijon mustard

¼ cup (60 ml) red wine vinegar

Leaves of ½ small bunch basil

Fronds of ½ small bunch dill

Leaves of ½ small bunch fresh mint

Leaves of ½ small bunch flat-leaf parsley

½ cup (87 g) capers, drained

½ cup (120 ml) extra-virgin olive oil

Kosher salt and freshly ground black pepper

FISH

Four 6-ounce (170-g) skinless sea bass fillets

Kosher salt and freshly ground black pepper

1 tablespoon (15 ml) extra-virgin olive oil

SPINACH

2 tablespoons (30 ml) extra-virgin olive oil

1 large bunch spinach (about 12 ounces/340 g), tough stems trimmed

Kosher salt and freshly ground black pepper

Juice of ½ lemon

For the sauce, combine the garlic, anchovy fillets, mustard, and vinegar in a food processor fitted with the metal blade. Pulse until the ingredients are finely chopped. Add the basil, dill, mint, parsley, and capers and pulse until the herbs are finely chopped. With the food processor running, add the olive oil in a thin stream and process until the sauce is smooth. Season to taste with salt and pepper. Set aside.

For the sea bass, heat a large nonstick skillet over medium-high heat. Season the fish on both sides with salt and pepper. Add the olive oil and swirl to coat the bottom of the pan. Add the fillets and brown on one side, 3 to 4 minutes. Flip, reduce the heat to medium-low, and cover the skillet. Cook until done to your liking, 4 to 6 minutes. Remove and keep warm.

For the spinach, return the skillet to medium-high heat and add the olive oil. Once the oil is hot, add the spinach and season with salt and pepper. Toss to coat the spinach in the oil. Cover and cook until the spinach wilts, about 2 minutes. Uncover, raise the heat to high, and cook away any excess liquid in the pan, 1 to 2 minutes. Drizzle with lemon juice.

To serve, make a bed of spinach on each individual serving plate. Top each with a fillet and top the fillets with the sauce.

Sautéed Cherry Tomatoes

Cherry tomatoes are wonderful as a salad, but when sautéed until juicy they make a tangy companion for fish.

• SERVES 6 •

2 tablespoons (30 ml) extra-virgin olive oil

1 pound (455 g) cipollini onions, peeled and trimmed (optional)

2 pints (1 lb/455 g) red and yellow cherry tomatoes

Sea salt and freshly ground black pepper

In a large skillet, heat the oil over medium heat. Add the onions, if using, stir to coat, then cover the skillet and cook until the onions are softened, 5 to 7 minutes. Add the tomatoes and season with salt and pepper. Stir to coat, cover the skillet, and cook approximately 10 minutes, until the tomatoes are soft and beginning to burst.

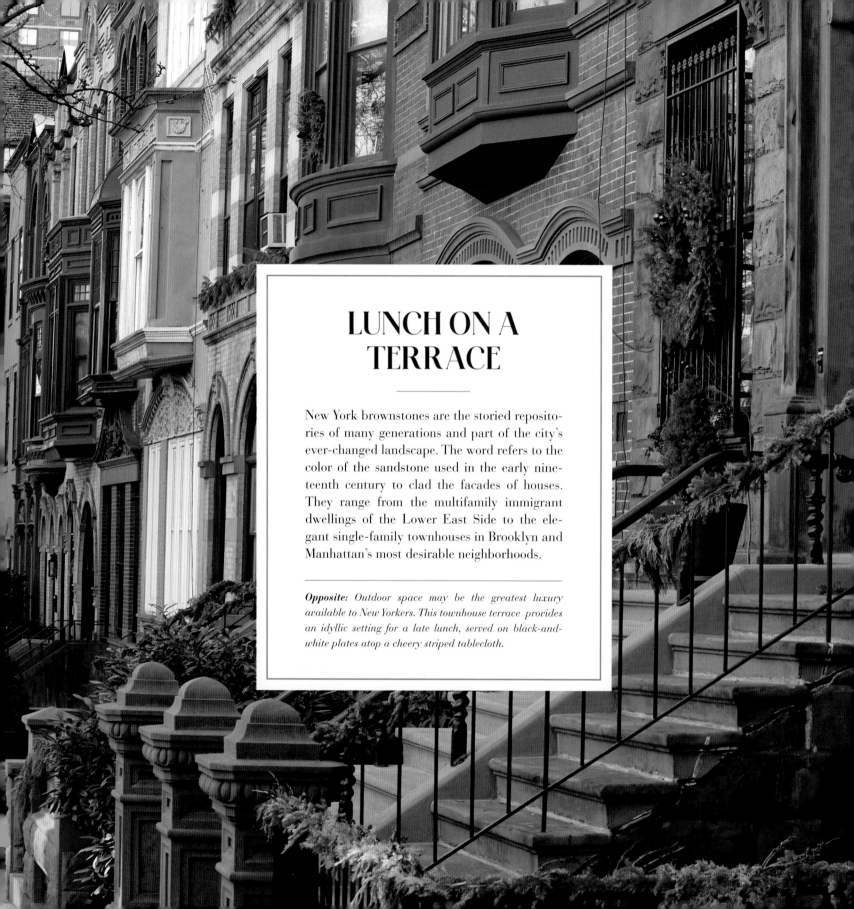

LUNCH ON A TERRACE

New York brownstones are the storied repositories of many generations and part of the city's ever-changed landscape. The word refers to the color of the sandstone used in the early nineteenth century to clad the facades of houses. They range from the multifamily immigrant dwellings of the Lower East Side to the elegant single-family townhouses in Brooklyn and Manhattan's most desirable neighborhoods.

Opposite: Outdoor space may be the greatest luxury available to New Yorkers. This townhouse terrace provides an idyllic setting for a late lunch, served on black-and-white plates atop a cheery striped tablecloth.

Pork Loin Stuffed
with Prunes, Walnuts & Bacon

The pork tenderloin is a cut from the area between the shoulder and back legs of the pig. A stuffing of dried fruit, walnuts, and bacon balances sweet and savory.

• SERVES 8 •

¼ cup (60 ml) extra-virgin olive oil

3 shallots, thinly sliced

8 strips bacon, chopped

6 ounces (170 g) cremini mushrooms, thinly sliced

3½ cups (430 g) pitted prunes or dried apricots, chopped

¼ cup (35 g) dried cherries

¼ cup (35 g) raisins

¼ cup (25 g) walnuts

¼ cup (10 g) fresh flat-leaf parsley, chopped

1¼ teaspoons (6 g) kosher salt

½ teaspoon (2 g) freshly ground black pepper

One 2½-pound (1.2-kg) pork tenderloin, silver skin removed

Preheat the oven to 400°F/205°C.

In a medium ovenproof skillet, heat 2 tablespoons (30 ml) of the oil over medium heat. Add the shallots and cook, stirring occasionally, until translucent, about 4 minutes. Add the bacon and cook, stirring occasionally, until browned, 3 to 4 minutes. Add the mushrooms and continue to cook until the mushrooms start to soften, about 3 minutes. Add the prunes, cherries, raisins, walnuts, and parsley and cook, stirring, until soft, about 5 minutes. Season with ¼ teaspoon (1 g) salt and ¼ teaspoon (1 g) pepper. Cook for 1 additional minute, stirring constantly. Transfer to a plate and set aside. Wipe out the skillet and reserve.

Using a sharp knife, cut a slit all the way down the long end of the tenderloin, making sure not to cut all the way through. Open the tenderloin like a book. Cover the pork with a piece of plastic wrap and pound it with the flat side of a meat mallet until about ¼ inch (6.5 mm) thick, taking care not to tear the meat.

With a spoon, spread the mushroom mixture evenly over the surface of the meat, leaving a ½ inch (1.2 cm) border free on all sides.

Roll up the meat tightly, jelly-roll style, and truss with twine or secure with 6 to 7 toothpicks. (Try to poke the toothpicks through parallel to one another to create a flat cooking surface.) Season all over with the remaining 1 teaspoon (5 g) salt and ¼ teaspoon (1 g) pepper.

Heat the remaining 2 tablespoons (30 ml) oil in the reserved skillet over medium heat. Once the oil is hot, add the pork seam-side or toothpick-side down and sear until browned all over, about 2 minutes per side. Transfer the skillet to the oven and roast until the pork is just cooked through and an instant-read thermometer registers 145°F/62°C in the thickest part of the meat, 18 to 20 minutes.

Transfer the pork to a cutting board, brush with any pan drippings, and allow to rest for 10 minutes before removing twine or toothpicks and slicing.

Roasted Root Vegetables

Root vegetables offer a fantastic variety of colorful, healthy, hearty, and crisp options. Delicious and homey, these power-houses of energy make any meal more memorable. And everyone has a favorite.

• SERVES 8 •

1 pound (455 g) carrots, cut into 2-inch (5-cm) sticks

3 Vidalia onions, cut into 1-inch (2.5-cm) cubes

2 large potatoes, peeled and cut into in 1-inch (2.5-cm) cubes

2 turnips, peeled and cut into in 1-inch (2.5-cm) cubes

1 large sweet potato, peeled and cut into 1-inch (2.5-cm) cubes

½ butternut squash, peeled, seeded, and cut into in 1-inch (2.5-cm) cubes

½ cup (120 ml) extra-virgin olive oil

Leaves of 5 sprigs fresh thyme

1½ teaspoons (7 g) kosher salt

Freshly ground black pepper

1 stick (8 tablespoons/113 g) unsalted butter, at room temperature

Preheat the oven to 400°F/205°C.

On a large baking sheet, combine the carrots, onions, potatoes, turnips, sweet potato, and squash. Add the oil and toss to coat. Mix in the thyme, salt, and pepper. With your hands, break the butter into pieces and scatter over the vegetables. Cover the baking sheet tightly with foil to stop steam from escaping.

Roast the vegetables until tender enough to pierce with a paring knife, about 40 minutes. Remove the foil, toss the vegetables, and return to the oven uncovered. Roast until golden brown, about 20 additional minutes.

Baguette
with Melted Chocolate & Fresh Lavender Butter

Bread and chocolate is one of the great delights of child-hood. Lavender adds a grown-up twist to those cherished memories.

• SERVES 4 •

1 stick (8 tablespoons/113 g) unsalted butter, at room temperature

1½ teaspoons (1.5 g) edible dried lavender flowers

2 (3-ounce/85-g) bars 64% dark chocolate, broken into pieces

1 baguette

Preheat the oven to 325°F/165°C.

In a small bowl, mash together the butter and lavender with a fork until well combined.

Cut the baguette crosswise on an angle into 4 pieces, then cut each piece lengthwise so you have cut bread for 4 sandwiches. Spread each piece with some lavender butter, then top with pieces of chocolate in a single layer.

Place the bread on a baking sheet and toast in the oven until the bread is golden brown and the chocolate and butter are melted, 6 to 8 minutes. Serve open-faced or sandwich pieces together in pairs before serving.

Jacques Lieberman

When asked about the best things about New York, Maribel does not hesitate, "SoHo, art, and my husband, Jacques. From the beginning, I started highlighting my husband Jacques Lieberman's artwork. His canvases are abstract and mesmerizing. With bold strokes and full of color, they are strikingly modern."

Maribel continues, "I use his designs on my ganache chocolates. His extraordinary life story, how he overcame a tragic childhood with grace and beauty, and the inspired vision that guided him. These qualities are still very much a part of what drives me forward."

Above: Some years ago, somewhere, Maribel and Jacques. Opposite: Original designs by Jacques atop ganache chocolates by Maribel.

DINING IN LOCUST VALLEY

Locust Valley, located thirty miles from Manhattan, became a stop on the Long Island Railroad in 1869. Wealthy magnates quickly discovered the area and began building luxurious mansions in the surrounding countryside. F. Scott Fitzgerald was a frequent visitor in the 1920s, and Locust Valley inspired the setting for his classic novel, *The Great Gatsby*.

In keeping with the summertime mood in this elegant home, an appetizer of assorted canapes is served al fresco. **Opposite:** *The dining room is set for guests and opens onto a charming sunroom bathed in light.*

Salmon Tartare
with Cilantro

This match made in heaven combines two textures and colors—the softness of pink salmon flesh with crisp green cilantro leaves. While cilantro is the name for the plant's leaves and stem, coriander is the name used for its dried seeds. If desired, this can be served on toasted bread as a passed hors d'oeuvre. This recipe makes enough to top about 30 toasts or crostini.

• SERVES 4 •

Juice of 1 lemon

½ medium white onion, finely diced

¼ cup (60 ml) extra-virgin olive oil

1 tablespoon (15 g) grainy mustard

1 pound (455 g) sushi-grade skinless wild salmon, cut into small dice

2 tablespoons (15 g) capers, drained

1 jalapeño pepper, seeded and finely chopped

½ bunch cilantro, finely chopped, plus whole leaves for garnish

4 sprigs fresh dill, chopped, optional

Kosher salt and freshly ground black pepper

In a small bowl, combine the lemon juice with ¼ cup (60 ml) water. Add the onion and soak at room temperature for 1 hour; drain.

In another small bowl, whisk together the oil and mustard with a fork until emulsified.

In a medium bowl, combine the salmon, onion, capers, jalapeño, chopped cilantro, and dill, if using. Gently toss to combine. Season to taste with salt and pepper and garnish with cilantro leaves.

Tiradito
with Chiles & Citrus Dressing

A gold-and-silver-themed table setting highlights the delicate colors of salmon tartare and tiradito. Tiradito is a wonderful way to start a meal. Its citrus dressing and spicy chiles enhance the freshness of thinly sliced raw fish and awaken the palate.

• SERVES 4 TO 6 •

18 ounces (510 g) sashimi-grade firm white fish, thinly sliced lengthwise

1 jalapeño pepper, seeded and thinly sliced

1 serrano pepper, seeded and thinly sliced

¼ medium red onion or 2 shallots, thinly sliced, optional

Juice of 4 lemons

Extra-virgin olive oil, for drizzling

Coarse sea salt and freshly ground black pepper

¼ cup cilantro leaves, optional

Lime wedges, for serving, optional

Arrange the fish on a ceramic or glass platter. Scatter on the jalapeño and serrano peppers, and the onion, if desired. Drizzle with the lemon juice and oil. Season with salt and pepper. Sprinkle with cilantro, if using, and serve with lime wedges, if desired.

Note: When preparing dishes that contain raw fish, make sure to use sashimi-grade fish. Consuming raw fish can be dangerous to certain individuals.

Roasted Duck Breast

Although the first published recipe for duck à l'orange is found in Louis Eustache Ude's 1813 cookbook, *The French Cook*, the dish continues to evolve. This delightfully creative and Asian-inflected interpretation is flavored with honey, mustard, ginger, soy sauce, and vinegar.

• SERVES 4 •

DUCK

1¼ cups (300 ml) soy sauce

One 2-inch (5-cm) piece fresh ginger, peeled and minced

2 tablespoons (40 g) honey

4 cloves garlic, finely chopped

1 large bunch cilantro, stems and leaves finely chopped

Four 8–10 ounce (250–280 g) duck breasts, skin on

1 tablespoon (15 ml) extra-virgin olive oil

SAUCE

2 sticks plus 4 tablespoons (20 tablespoons/280 g) unsalted butter, cut into small cubes

3 cloves garlic, chopped

½ medium yellow or white onion, chopped

½ cup (120 ml) raspberry vinegar

4 cups (960 ml) freshly squeezed orange juice

Kosher salt and freshly ground black pepper

1 tablespoon honey

1 teaspoon grainy mustard

To make the duck, whisk together the soy sauce, ginger, honey, garlic, and cilantro in a large bowl or baking dish. Add the duck, toss to coat, and refrigerate, covered, for at least 8 hours and up to 12 hours.

One hour before cooking, remove the duck from the refrigerator and let it come to room temperature.

In a large cast-iron skillet, heat the oil over medium heat. Add the duck skin-side down and cook until the skin is crisp and golden brown and the fat is rendered, 8 to 12 minutes; spoon off excess fat as it collects. Turn the duck and continue to cook to desired doneness. An instant-read thermometer will register 135°F to 140°F/57°C to 60°C for medium-rare. Remove the duck from the pan and set aside to rest at room temperature while you make the sauce.

To make the sauce, drain excess fat from the skillet, add 1 tablespoon of the butter, and melt over medium heat. Add the garlic and onion and cook, stirring and scraping up the browned bits in the pan, until translucent, about 3 minutes. Add the vinegar and reduce by half. Add the orange juice and cook, stirring, until reduced by two-thirds, 5 to 7 additional minutes. Season to taste with salt and pepper.

Incorporate the remaining butter, a few pieces at a time, whisking until melted and smooth. Strain the sauce through a fine-mesh sieve into a small clean skillet and set over low heat. Add the honey and mustard and mix well. Remove from the heat but keep warm. Thinly slice the duck and serve with the warm sauce on the side.

Beet Puree

Beets are believed to have originated in the Mediterranean and spread eastward in prehistoric times. Today, they are a widely cultivated root vegetable that thrives in cool weather. They are referred to as beetroots in English-speaking countries other than the United States. This dish (pictured in top right hand-corner of the image opposite) pairs nicely with Crêpes Suzette served with crème fraîche (see recipe, page 84).

• SERVES 4 TO 6 •

6 medium beets, peeled and quartered

2 tablespoons (30 g) crème fraîche

¼ cup (25 g) walnuts

Arrange a steamer basket in a large pot filled with several inches of water and bring to a boil over high heat. Add the beets, cover, and steam until they are tender enough to pierce with a paring knife, about 20 minutes.

Remove from the heat and allow to cool slightly. Transfer the beets to a blender, reserving the steaming liquid, and puree until smooth. Thin to the desired consistency by adding the steaming liquid in small amounts. Add the crème fraîche and blend to combine.

Transfer the mixture to a serving bowl and scatter the walnuts on the surface.

Above, left to right: Coffee with a selection of MarieBelle chocolates; a close-up of MarieBelle's chocolate ganaches; tea with chocolate confections.

A WHITE
SATIN EVENING

French accents, including elegant gold and silver tableware and crystal glassware, define the decor of this sophisticated loft. Maribel's stylish home is a reminder of the important role played by France in America's history, including French art and cultural contributions to the ethos of New York, and of course the city's landmark the Statue of Liberty.

Opposite: High ceilings, tall tapers, and white linens strike a chic mood for an elegant evening.

Cucumber & Tequila Cocktail

Although fermented agave was an ancient and revered drink in pre-Columbian Mexico, it was a new distillation technique refined by the Spanish that produced agave wine, which in the early twentieth century was officially renamed tequila.

• 1 SERVING •

3 ounces (90 ml) freshly squeezed cucumber juice

1 ounce (30 ml) freshly squeezed lime juice

2 ounces (60 ml) white tequila

½ teaspoon (2 g) sugar

¼ cup (60 g) ice, plus more for serving

3 ounces (90 ml) sparkling water, such as San Pellegrino, or club soda

1 sprig mint

In a cocktail shaker, combine the cucumber and lime juices, tequila, sugar, and ice, and shake well.

Strain the mixture into a chilled tumbler filled with ice and top off with sparkling water. Garnish with the mint.

Skinny Margarita

The margarita is a sour, a family of cocktails that contain liquor, an acidic element (typically a citrus juice like lemon or lime juice), and a sweetener. The first-known published recipe for a tequila sour—the predecessor of the margarita—appeared in barman Charlie Connolly's book, *The World-Famous Cotton Club: 1939 Book of Mixed Drinks.*

• 1 SERVING •

2 lime wedges

Salt for glass rim

1 cup (240 g) ice, plus more for serving

Juice of 1 lime

2 ounces (60 ml) white tequila

2 ounces (60 ml) club soda

Rub the rim of a rocks glass with 1 lime wedge and dip it in salt. Fill with ice.

In a cocktail shaker, combine the lime juice, tequila, and ice. Shake well until chilled. Strain the mixture into the salt-rimmed glass. Top with the club soda.

Garnish with the remaining lime wedge.

Citrus-Infused Fish Fillet
with Grilled Tomatillos & Arugula Sprouts

Microgreens, such as arugula sprouts, enhance the taste, texture, and appearance of a dish. Here, microgreens and grilled tomatillos provide the perfect counterpoint to a light fish recipe that highlights peppery and citrus tones.

• SERVES 6 •

SOFRITO

1 large Spanish onion, quartered

1 large tomato, quartered

½ green bell pepper, seeded and quartered

½ jalapeño pepper, seeded and halved

2 tablespoons (30 ml) extra-virgin olive oil

Kosher salt and freshly ground black pepper

SAUCE, TOMATILLOS, AND FISH

2 tablespoons (30 ml) extra-virgin olive oil

½ yellow bell pepper, seeded and diced

½ jalapeño pepper, seeded and finely chopped

10 ounces (280 g) yellow cherry tomatoes, quartered

4 tomatillos, husked, halved, and sliced into half-moons

6 (6 oz/170 g) skinless white fish fillets, such as sea bass

Kosher salt and freshly ground white pepper

2 ounces (55 g) arugula sprouts

Peeled lime wedges, for serving

For the sofrito, combine the onion, tomato, green bell pepper, and jalapeño in a food processor fitted with the metal blade and pulse until finely chopped but not perfectly smooth. In a medium saucepan, heat the oil over medium heat. Add the vegetable mixture and cook, stirring occasionally, until slightly reduced, about 10 minutes. Season with salt and pepper to taste. Force through a sieve or process with a food mill and set aside.

For the sauce, heat 1 tablespoon (15 ml) of the oil in a small skillet over medium heat. Add the red bell pepper and jalapeño and cook, stirring occasionally, until just beginning to soften, about 3 minutes. Add the tomatoes and cook until soft and bursting, about 5 additional minutes.

For the tomatillos, brush a grill pan with the remaining 1 tablespoon (15 ml) oil and place over medium heat. Cook the tomatillos until softened and browning, about 3 minutes per side.

For the fish, season the fillets with salt and white pepper.

Spread the sofrito in the bottom of a large skillet with a tight-fitting lid. Add the fish, cover the pan, and cook over very low heat until the fish is cooked through, about 10 minutes.

To serve, spoon a little of the pureed sofrito on the bottom of the plate. (If you wish, reserve any leftover sofrito for another use. It will keep in the refrigerator for 3 days.). Slice the fish and place it on top. Spoon some of the pepper-tomato sauce over the fish. Serve with the tomatillos, arugula sprouts, and lime wedges.

Seared Filet Mignon
with Roasted Maitake Mushrooms & Fennel

Fresh herbs not only look elegant as garnishes for this traditional filet mignon, but their flavor enhances it greatly. Sweet fennel and earthy mushrooms round out this satisfying dish.

• SERVES 6 •

BEEF

Six 6- to 8-ounce (170- to 225-g) filet mignon steaks

2 sticks (16 tablespoons/ 225 g) unsalted butter, at room temperature

1 shallot, finely chopped

Leaves of 2 sprigs fresh rosemary, finely chopped

½ teaspoon (2.5 g) kosher salt, plus more to taste

Freshly ground black pepper to taste

2 tablespoons (30 ml) extra-virgin olive oil

VEGETABLES

8 ounces (225 g) maitake mushrooms, thickly sliced

8 ounces (225 g) oyster mushrooms, thickly sliced

Leaves of 2 sprigs fresh rosemary, minced

Leaves of 2 sprigs fresh thyme

3 cloves garlic, sliced

¼ cup plus 1 tablespoon (75 ml) extra-virgin olive oil

Kosher salt and freshly ground black pepper

1 medium bulb fennel, halved, cored, and sliced ¼-inch thick

Sprigs fresh bay leaves and fresh thyme, for garnish

Remove the steaks from the refrigerator 30 minutes to 1 hour before you plan to cook them to bring to room temperature. Preheat the oven to 375°F/190°C with racks in the upper and lower thirds.

Combine the butter, shallot, rosemary, ½ teaspoon (2.5 g) salt, and a generous amount of pepper. Mash with a fork to combine. Spread into a ramekin and refrigerate until ready to use.

Meanwhile, for the vegetables, place the mushrooms on a baking sheet with half of the rosemary leaves, thyme leaves, and garlic. Drizzle with 3 tablespoons (45 ml) olive oil and season with salt and pepper. Toss to combine and spread in a single layer. On a second baking sheet, toss the fennel with the remaining 2 tablespoons (30 ml) olive oil and the remaining rosemary, thyme, and garlic. Season with salt and pepper and spread in a single layer. Roast, rotating the sheets from front to back and top to bottom halfway through, until the vegetables are browned and tender, 15 to 20 minutes. Leave the oven on.

For the steaks, heat a large cast-iron skillet over high heat until very hot, at least 2 minutes. Put the steaks on a plate, drizzle with the 2 tablespoons (30 ml) olive oil, and season well with salt and pepper. Sear the steaks in the pan until browned and crusty, then flip and sear the second sides, about 2 minutes per side. Transfer the skillet to the oven and roast until the steak is done to your liking, 4 to 6 minutes for rare to medium-rare (depending on the thickness of your steaks). Remove to a cutting board and let rest for a few minutes. Top each steak with a knob of the compound butter and serve with the mushrooms and fennel. Garnish with thyme and bay leaf sprigs.

Roasted Sweet Potato Chips

Known as *batata* in the indigenous Taino language or *papa* in Quechua, the sweet potato is an ancient cultivar native to the tropical areas of Central and South America. It was only introduced into European kitchens in the sixteenth century, following the Spanish conquests.

• SERVES 6 •

2 medium sweet potatoes (1 to 1½ pounds/455 to 680 g)

¼ cup (60 ml) garlic-infused olive oil

1 teaspoon (5 g) kosher salt, plus more to taste

Freshly ground black pepper

Preheat the oven to 450°F/230°C with racks in the upper and lower thirds. Slice the sweet potatoes on a mandoline into disks about ¼ inch (3 mm) thick. Put the sweet potatoes in a large bowl and drizzle with the olive oil. Season with 1 teaspoon (5 g) salt and a generous amount of pepper. Toss to coat evenly.

Spread the slices in a single layer on baking sheets. Roast, flipping the slices halfway through and rotating the sheets front to back and top to bottom, until they are browned and crisp on the edges, 12 to 15 minutes.

Remove to a plate lined with paper towels to drain. Adjust seasoning with additional salt and pepper and serve warm.

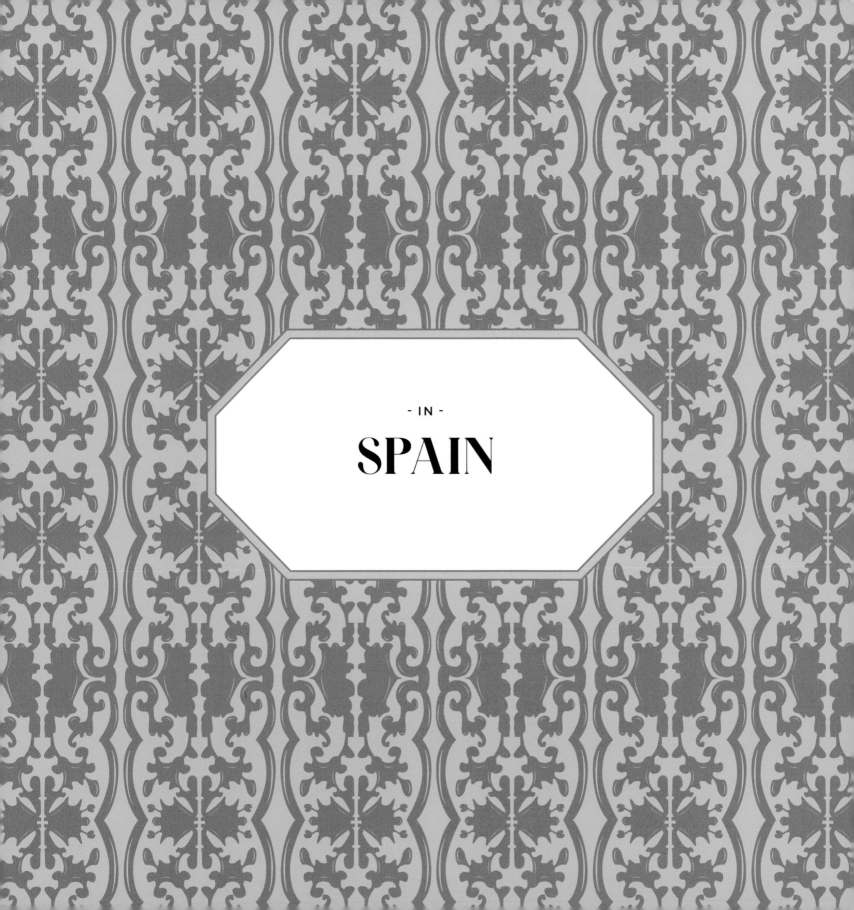

- IN -

SPAIN

The cuisines of the Iberian Peninsula are a rich tapestry of distinct identities. Invaded in 206 BC, the peninsula became a province of the Roman Empire for 700 years. In 711, the Islamic Empire conquered most of the peninsula, ruling over Al-Andalus for 800 years.

Then, starting in the late fifteenth century, following the Battle of Granada and the restoration of a Catholic monarchy, the Spanish throne embarked on a number of expeditions to the New World in search of gold, spices, and new lands—a venture that led to the introduction in Europe of Native American crops such as potatoes, corn, and tomatoes, as well as cacao. Today, Spanish cuisine is a cornucopia of earthy and complex dishes, many of which incorporate those American imports.

MARIBEL'S MENUS

(recipes in roman are provided)

OF CHOCOLATE AND TRADITIONS
Aragon

MarieBelle's Hot Chocolate . . . 18 · Cinnamon-Infused Churros with Chocolate Drizzle . . . 124
Melted Dark Chocolate for Dipping . . . 124

WITHIN WHITE WALLS
Mahón, Menorca

Ensalada Nizarda . . . 128

A LATE SUMMER CELEBRATION
Mahón, Menorca

Albariño or Other White Wine · *Salad of Lettuce, String Beans & Tomatoes*
Citrus & Seafood Escabeche with Red Pepper . . . 134
Grilled Dorado & Pineapple with Cilantro . . . 137 · *Fried Green Plantains*

PICNIC FOR AN AFTERNOON SAIL
Port of Mahón, Menorca

Rioja Rosado · *Tapas: Stuffed Olives, Peppers, Baby Shrimp Skewers, Anchovies & Salumi*
Picadito of Duck Confit with Prunes . . . 140 · Shrimp & Pineapple Salad . . . 143
Tropical Fruit: Sliced Pineapple, Papaya & Mango

OF TAPAS AND MENORCA
Es Castell, Menorca

Mencia or Other Red Wine · Zucchini & Potato Tortilla . . . 146
Fried Eggplant with Honey . . . 149 · Andalusian Migas . . . 149

A FISHERMAN'S FEAST
Sant Lluís, Menorca

Zinfandel Rosé · *Pinot Noir or Other Light Red Wine*
Endive & Fig Salad . . . 152 · Stuffed Tomatoes . . . 155 · Tortilla Española . . . 156
Grilled Sardines . . . 157 · Grilled Shrimp . . . 157 · *Peperonata* · *Roasted Garlic*

A SUNSET SUPPER
Sant Lluís, Menorca

Txakoli or Other Dry White Wine · *Roasted Suckling Pig* · *Raw Green Cabbage*
Caramelized Figs . . . 162 · *Dimitri's Flourless Chocolate Cake*
Flourless Orange-Almond Cake with Chocolate Topping . . . 163

DINING WITH LEGENDS
Cadaqués

Kiwi Caipiroska · *Strawberry Gin Smash* · *Vinho Verde* · Clams with Garlic & Wine . . . 168
Bacalao Sautéed with Wine & Tomatoes · Coca de Vidre . . . 171 · Crema Catalana con Ananas . . . 172

---

*Opposite: This charming port on the island of Menorca is lined with leisure and fishing boats. **Following pages, clockwise from left:** Exterior of a Menorcan home; the bell tower of the fishing village of Binibeca Vell on Menorca; al fresco dining on the island; tropical fruits by a Menorcan bay; paella with langoustines, clams, and mussels.*

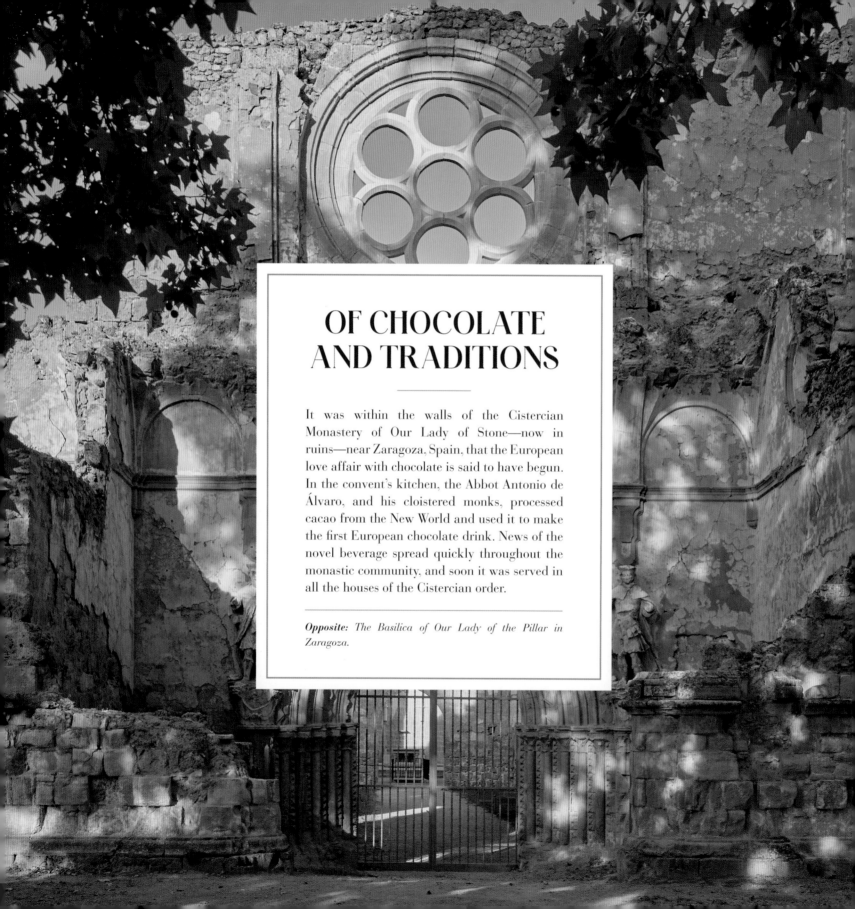

OF CHOCOLATE AND TRADITIONS

It was within the walls of the Cistercian Monastery of Our Lady of Stone—now in ruins—near Zaragoza, Spain, that the European love affair with chocolate is said to have begun. In the convent's kitchen, the Abbot Antonio de Álvaro, and his cloistered monks, processed cacao from the New World and used it to make the first European chocolate drink. News of the novel beverage spread quickly throughout the monastic community, and soon it was served in all the houses of the Cistercian order.

Opposite: The Basilica of Our Lady of the Pillar in Zaragoza.

Cinnamon-Infused Churros
with Chocolate Drizzle

Opposite, hot chocolate and churros in front of the Monastery of Our Lady of Stone in Aragon, Spain. Churros, a delicious fried dough creation, are often dipped in thick hot chocolate. Here we drizzle on the chocolate, just for fun.

• MAKES 12 CHURROS •

1 cup (125 g) all-purpose flour

Pinch kosher salt

1 cup (240 ml) Cinnamon-Infused Water (recipe follows)

1 teaspoon (3 g) sugar

1½ tablespoons (20 g) unsalted butter

2 large eggs

1 teaspoon (5 ml) pure vanilla extract

Vegetable or canola oil, for frying

Melted Dark Chocolate for Dipping (recipe follows)

Sift the flour into a large bowl. Mix in the salt with a spoon.

Place the cinnamon water in a medium saucepan over medium-high heat and bring to a boil. Add the sugar and stir until dissolved, about 2 minutes. Add the butter and the flour mixture and stir until combined. Remove from the heat and let the mixture cool for 2 minutes.

In a small bowl, beat the eggs with an electric mixer on medium-high for 2 minutes. Add the eggs to the flour mixture and stir to combine. Stir in the vanilla extract.

Line a plate with paper towels and set aside. Fit a piping bag with a ¾-inch (2-cm) tip. Fill the bag with the batter.

Add enough oil to a heavy 8-inch (20-cm) skillet to go about 2 inches (5 cm) up the sides and set over high heat. Bring to 325°F/165°C. Working in batches to avoid crowding the pan, pipe the batter in logs 5 to 6 inches (12.7 to 15.25 cm) long into the hot oil.

Fry until golden brown, about 1½ minutes. With a slotted spoon or skimmer, transfer to the prepared plate. Repeat with the remaining batter, adding more oil to the skillet as needed. Serve piping hot with the chocolate drizzled over them.

Cinnamon-Infused Water

• MAKES 1 CUP •

1 cinnamon stick

2 whole cloves

Combine 1½ cups (360 ml) water, the cinnamon stick, and cloves in a small saucepan. Bring to a boil over high heat and reduce to 1 cup (240 ml). Strain and allow to cool to room temperature before using.

Melted Dark Chocolate for Dipping

• MAKES 1 CUP •

½ cup (100 g) chopped 70% dark chocolate or dark chocolate chips

½ cup (120 ml) heavy cream

Place the chocolate and cream in a heatproof bowl and microwave in 30-second bursts, stirring in between, until smooth. Alternatively, heat the heavy cream in the top of a double boiler (or a heatproof bowl set over a pot of simmering water), then add the chocolate and stir until melted and smooth. Set aside for 5 minutes to cool and thicken slightly.

WITHIN WHITE WALLS

Menorca's marés stone is omnipresent. From the island's prehistoric monuments to its fortresses and churches, it is still used today for buildings. Even the walls of the Balearic donkey pens are often made of this sandstone. Following a custom from the fifteenth century, when houses were whitewashed with lime as protection against disease, today's homes still embrace white walls but to guard against the sun's heat.

Opposite: The shaded outdoor sitting dining area of this charming home, ringed by Menorca's wild greenery and a massive marés sandstone wall, provides the perfect frame for a low-key table design.

Ensalada Nizarda

In 1972, Jacques Médecin, the mayor of Nice, wrote that either anchovies or canned tuna could be used to make the city's famed salade niçoise. In Spain, which boasts some of the world's best canned seafood, the latter option caught on like wildfire.

• SERVES 6 TO 8 •

Kosher salt

9 new potatoes, about 1 pound (455 g)

2 pounds (1 kg) haricots verts, blanched

10 plum tomatoes, halved

½ cup (120 g) pitted Niçoise olives

1 teaspoon (5 g) coarsely ground black pepper

¾ cup (180 ml) Champagne or White Wine Vinaigrette (recipe follows)

1 head bibb lettuce, leaves separated and left whole

6 hard-boiled eggs, peeled and quartered lengthwise

One 12-ounce (340-g) can or jar of oil-packed white tuna, drained

Bring a large pot of salted water to a boil and cook the potatoes until tender enough to pierce with a paring knife, 10 to 12 minutes. Drain and set aside to cool. When the potatoes are cool enough to handle, peel and slice them and place the slices in a large bowl.

Add the haricots verts, tomatoes, olives, 1 teaspoon (5 g) salt, and the pepper. Pour the vinaigrette over the vegetables and toss gently.

Line a platter with the lettuce leaves. Place the potato mixture on the lettuce, then scatter on the egg wedges. Flake the tuna on top of the salad. Serve at room temperature.

Champagne or White Wine Vinaigrette

• MAKES ¾ CUP (180 ML) •

1 tablespoon (15 g) Dijon mustard

¼ cup (60 ml) Champagne or white wine vinegar

½ small shallot, minced

½ teaspoon (.5 g) minced tarragon leaves

½ teaspoon (2.5 g) kosher salt

¼ teaspoon (1 g) coarsely ground black pepper

½ cup (120 ml) extra-virgin olive oil

In a small bowl, whisk together the mustard, vinegar, shallot, tarragon, salt, and pepper. While whisking, add the olive oil in a thin stream. Whisk until the vinaigrette is emulsified.

Above, left to right: Maribel making her signature chocolate sauce (page 124); a charming dishware cabinet on Menorca; boiling water for tea; monumental stones dating to Menorca's Talaiotic period, around 2000 BCE.

A LATE SUMMER CELEBRATION

Inhabited since the Stone Age—by many of history's great civilizations, from the Carthaginians to the Romans and the Moors—Menorca has seen plenty of celebrations. Today, as friends gather in the waning days of summer, the mood is imbued with a sense of gratitude as we celebrate the warm welcome, and natural wonders, that the island bestows upon its visitors.

Opposite: Maribel greets her guests with a seafood escabeche (page 134), a popular culinary dish of summer gatherings.

Citrus & Seafood Escabeche
with Red Pepper

Escabeche is a perfect summer dish. The Spanish adopted escabeche from Peru, where ceviche, a dish of fish macerated in vinegar or citrus, was made as far back as 2,000 years ago.

• SERVES 6 •

8 ounces (225 g) bay scallops, halved through the middle

8 ounces (225 g) corvina or sea bass fillets, cut into ½-inch (1.25-cm) dice

1 medium red onion, cut into small dice

About 1 cup (240 ml) freshly squeezed lime juice

8 ounces (225 g) medium shrimp, peeled and deveined

1 jalapeño pepper, seeded and minced

1 red bell pepper, seeded and diced

½ mango, peeled, pitted, and diced

½ cup (20 g) fresh cilantro leaves, chopped

2 tablespoons (30 ml) freshly squeezed orange juice

1 tablespoon (15 ml) extra-virgin olive oil

Kosher salt and freshly ground black pepper

1 pink grapefruit, peeled and supremed

1 orange, peeled and supremed

2 limes, peeled and supremed

In a large bowl, combine the scallops, corvina, onion, and enough lime juice to cover the ingredients. Cover the bowl and refrigerate, stirring occasionally, for 2 to 3 hours.

Meanwhile, bring a medium saucepan of water to a boil. Add the shrimp and cook over medium-high heat until opaque, 1 to 2 minutes. Transfer to a large bowl of ice water to cool, then drain and cut each shrimp into 3 or 4 pieces.

Drain most of the liquid from the marinated fish. Transfer the fish to a serving bowl. Add the jalapeño, bell pepper, mango, cilantro, orange juice, and olive oil. Season with salt and pepper and toss to combine.

Arrange the grapefruit, orange, and lime segments over the ceviche. Refrigerate until ready to serve.

Grilled Dorado & Pineapple
with Cilantro

Mahi mahi, known as dorado in Spain, is a sturdy yet tender fish that stands up well to grilling.

• SERVES 4 •

1 clove garlic

One 3-inch (7.5-cm) piece ginger, peeled and coarsely chopped

1 jalapeño pepper, seeded and coarsely chopped

1 stalk lemongrass, coarsely chopped

½ large white onion, coarsely chopped

Leaves of 1 bunch cilantro, chopped

One 13.5-ounce (400-ml) can unsweetened coconut milk

3 tablespoons (45 ml) extra-virgin olive oil

Juice of 2 limes

About 1 teaspoon (5 g) kosher salt

1½ pounds (680 g) mahi mahi fillets, cut into 2-inch (5-cm) pieces

1 cup (210 g) 1½-inch (4-cm) cubes pineapple

In a food processor fitted with the metal blade, combine the garlic, ginger, jalapeño, lemongrass, and onion. Reserve some cilantro for garnish and add the rest to the food processor. Pulse until coarsely chopped and combined.

Add the coconut milk and 2 tablespoons (30 ml) of the olive oil and pulse to form a chunky mixture, about 1 minute. Add the lime juice. Taste and add salt.

In a medium bowl, toss the mahi mahi with the coconut milk mixture. Cover and refrigerate for 5 to 6 hours.

When you are ready to cook the fish, soak bamboo skewers in water for at least 20 minutes. Heat a grill or place a grill pan over medium heat.

Thread the fish and pineapple onto the skewers. Place the skewers on a baking sheet, drizzle with the remaining 1 tablespoon (15 ml) oil, and turn to coat.

Grill the skewers, covered, until grill marks form, about 2 minutes. Turn the skewers and continue to cook until the fish is cooked through, about 2 additional minutes. Garnish with the reserved cilantro before serving.

PICNIC FOR AN AFTERNOON SAIL

The timeless sound of gently rocking crafts that dot the port of this Balearic Island tells a thousand tales. Whether caressed by the summer's mild sea breezes, or buffeted by the northern Mistral from France, wind is truly the master that forged these islands and brought people and prosperity here.

Opposite: Spanish tapas, or appetizers, come in a variety of festive and delicious bite-size dishes that include stuffed olives and peppers, baby squid or shrimp, and tender shredded meats or chorizo. In fact, the possibilities are endless and the perfect choice to serve aboard a boat.

Picadito of Duck Confit
with Prunes

Vegetables, seafood, and meat can all be picadito, meaning shredded or chopped. Here, a tasty picadito of duck is served on toasts for a savory yet subtle treat.

• SERVES 4 TO 6 •

4 small confit duck legs, about 1 pound (455 g) total

4 ripe figs

5 pitted prunes, roughly chopped

Kosher salt

1 small baguette, sliced crosswise into about 16 rounds

Extra-virgin olive oil, for brushing

Preheat the oven to 325°F/165°C.

Set the duck legs, skin-side down, in a skillet where they fit in a single snug layer and place over medium-low heat. Cook until the fat has rendered and the duck is browned and tender, 3 to 4 minutes per side. Remove to a plate. When the duck is cool enough to handle, shred the meat by hand.

Pour off all but a thin film of the rendered duck fat from the skillet and place over medium heat. Add the figs and prunes and season with salt. Cook, stirring occasionally, until the figs have just softened but still hold their shape, 2 to 3 minutes. Remove the figs and place in the center of a serving platter. Stir in the duck and cook just to heat through, about 1 minute.

Meanwhile, place the baguette slices on a baking sheet and brush with olive oil. Bake until crisp and golden, 10 to 12 minutes. Remove from the oven and allow to cool slightly.

Top the toasts with the duck mixture and arrange around the figs. Serve warm.

Shrimp & Pineapple Salad

This summer seafood salad looks beautiful and tastes even better. The carved-out pineapple makes a playful serving vessel.

• SERVES 2 •

1 pineapple

12 large shrimp, peeled and deveined

20 cherry tomatoes, halved

4 radishes, sliced

1 seedless cucumber, peeled and thinly sliced

2 scallions, thinly sliced

¼ cup (25 g) thinly sliced red onion

1 small piece jalapeño pepper, seeded and thinly sliced

2 tablespoons Simple Vinaigrette (recipe follows)

12 mint leaves, cut into chiffonade

Scallion curls, for garnish

Halve the pineapple lengthwise. Hollow it out by separating the fruit from the peel. Reserve the shell. Core the flesh and slice into bite-size pieces.

Bring a medium saucepan of water to a boil. Add the shrimp and cook over medium-high heat until opaque, 1 to 2 minutes. Drain and reserve.

In a large bowl, combine the pineapple flesh, tomatoes, radishes, cucumber, scallions, onion, and jalapeño. Add the dressing and toss to combine. To serve, place the salad in the pineapple shells. Arrange the shrimp on top, garnish with mint and scallion curls, and serve.

Simple Vinaigrette

• MAKES ⅓ CUP (80 ML) •

2 tablespoons (30 ml) Champagne vinegar

1¼ teaspoons (6 g) Dijon mustard

¼ teaspoon (1 g) kosher salt

Freshly ground black pepper

⅓ cup (80 ml) extra-virgin olive oil

In a small bowl, whisk together the vinegar, mustard, salt, and pepper. While whisking, add the olive oil in a thin stream, then whisk until the dressing is emulsified. Store any leftover dressing in an airtight container in the refrigerator for up to 7 days.

OF TAPAS AND MENORCA

While fishing is key to the cuisine of Menorca, farming also plays an important role in its culinary landscape. An elaborate irrigation system introduced many centuries ago by the Moors is still in use today to grow many types of crops. Today, "dry farming" methods also allow farmers to grow an extensive variety of produce that includes melons, eggplants, tomatoes, onions, and lettuces, as well as grains.

Opposite: Hearty tapas to satisfy any appetite: Zucchini and Potato Tortilla (page 146), Tortilla Española (page 156), and Fried Eggplant with Honey (page 149).

Zucchini & Potato Tortilla

This variation on the traditional Spanish tortilla includes zucchini for a touch of sweetness. Serve it tapas-style in thin wedges. If you want to try the traditional version, see page 156.

• SERVES 6 •

6 to 8 small zucchini

1 teaspoon (5 g) kosher salt, plus more to taste

1 pound (455 g) Yukon Gold potatoes

1 cup (240 ml) extra-virgin olive oil

2 large white Spanish onions, cut into ¼-inch (6.5-mm) slices

Freshly ground black pepper

7 large eggs

Grate the zucchini on the largest holes of a box grater into a large bowl. Add the 1 teaspoon (5 g) salt, toss, and set aside for 30 minutes.

Meanwhile, peel the potatoes, and cut them into ⅓-inch (8.5-mm) slices.

Heat ½ cup (120 ml) of the oil in a large skillet over medium-high heat until hot, then add the potatoes and onions. Season to taste with salt and pepper. Reduce the heat to medium-low and cook, stirring occasionally, until the potatoes are almost tender but still firm in the center, about 30 minutes. Do not allow the potatoes and onions to brown. Adjust the heat if heatproof necessary.

Transfer the zucchini to a colander to drain, then squeeze small handfuls to remove as much liquid as possible. Add the zucchini to the potato mixture and cook, stirring occasionally, until the potatoes are tender and the zucchini is slightly browned, about 15 minutes.

Place a colander in a heatproof bowl and transfer the vegetable mixture to the colander to drain, reserving the oil. Cool for 5 minutes.

In a bowl, beat the eggs with a fork, then stir in the vegetables and 1 tablespoon (15 ml) of the reserved oil. Season with salt and pepper.

Heat the remaining ½ cup (120 ml) oil in the skillet and add the egg mixture. Press down with the back of a wooden spoon to make it flat and even. Cook, covered, over low heat until the top is almost set and the underside is golden, 12 to 15 minutes. Remove from the heat and let stand, covered, for 15 minutes.

Run a silicone spatula around the tortilla and shake the skillet to loosen (if the bottom sticks to the skillet, carefully slide the spatula underneath). Slide the tortilla out of the skillet onto a large flat plate, then overturn the skillet on top of the tortilla and invert the plate and the pan so the tortilla falls back into the skillet. Remove the plate. Cook over low heat, uncovered, until completely set, about 15 additional minutes.

Slide the tortilla onto a serving plate and cut it into wedges. Serve warm or at room temperature.

Fried Eggplant
with Honey

Long, thin Japanese eggplant are tender and have relatively few seeds, so they're less bitter than other varieties. Here they share a traditional terra-cotta serving dish with Andalusian Migas (recipe opposite).

• SERVES 6 •

4 Japanese eggplant, sliced at an angle into ¼ inch (6.5 mm) pieces

2 tablespoons (30 g) kosher salt, plus more to taste

2½ cups (600 ml) whole milk

Canola oil, for frying

1 cup (125 g) all-purpose flour, if using

3 tablespoons (60 g) honey

Finely grated lemon zest, for garnish

Place the eggplant slices in a single layer on a rack set over a baking sheet. Sprinkle with the 2 tablespoons (30 g) salt. Place another baking sheet on top of the eggplant slices and press firmly. Let stand for 20 minutes, then press once more. The goal is to extract as much liquid from the eggplant slices as possible. Transfer the eggplant slices to a large bowl and add the milk. Cover the bowl with plastic wrap and refrigerate for at least 2 hours or overnight.

When ready to cook, in a large enameled cast-iron casserole heat 1 inch (2.5 cm) oil to 350°F/175°C over medium-high heat.

Optional: Place the flour in a shallow bowl. Remove the eggplant slices from the milk, shaking off any excess liquid, and dredge them in the flour. Shake off excess flour.

Working in batches, fry the eggplant slices in the hot oil, turning a few times, until golden brown, about 3 minutes. With a slotted spoon or skimmer, transfer the eggplant to a baking sheet lined with paper towels and season with salt. Transfer the fried eggplant to a serving platter, drizzle with the honey, and sprinkle with lemon zest. Season with additional salt and serve immediately.

Andalusian Migas

Migas is pure anytime, anywhere food. Originally a Spanish breakfast dish, it is now also served at lunch or dinner—and varying types of migas are also eaten in Portugal and Mexico.

• SERVES 8 •

5 cups (500 g) stale bread cubes

3 tablespoons (45 ml) extra-virgin olive oil

1 pound (455 g) pork rind, cut into 1-inch (2.5-cm) strips

1 pound (455 g) chorizo, chopped

10 cloves garlic, peeled

Juice of ½ lemon

Kosher salt and freshly ground black pepper

Crumble the stale bread onto a large plate. Sprinkle with a small amount of water to moisten but not wet. Cover and allow to rest for 8 hours.

To prepare the migas, line a plate with paper towels. Place the oil in a large skillet over medium-high heat and cook the pork rind, stirring frequently, until golden brown, about 5 minutes. Add the chorizo and cook, stirring frequently, until it is golden brown, 7 to 10 minutes. Using a slotted spoon or skimmer, remove the chorizo and pork rind from the pan and transfer to the prepared plate to drain. Do not rinse the pan.

Add the garlic to the skillet and cook, stirring occasionally, over medium-high heat until golden, about 3 minutes. Add the breadcrumbs and lemon juice and stir to combine. Cook, stirring constantly, until the breadcrumbs are evenly toasted, about 10 minutes.

Return the pork rind and chorizo to the skillet and cook until warmed through, 5 to 7 minutes. Season with salt and pepper. Serve hot.

A FISHERMAN'S FEAST

Menorca's vibrant year-round villages are similar to those on other Balearic Islands. Here the land, the seasons, and the sea and its tides set the rhythms of daily life. While generations of farmers have grown their seasonal crops, fishermen have been casting their nets off the island's coast for more than a millennium.

Opposite: The varied geography of the island's coastline, with rocky seabeds and calm coves, makes it particularly fertile ground. The fish is fresh and fit for a feast. For this fun and festive outdoor meal, Maribel has paired blue-and-white serving dishes and white china with vibrant orange placemats and napkins and green glasses, which echo the surrounding greenery.

Endive & Fig Salad

Belgian endive is a small cylindrical head of lettuce with tightly packed yellow leaves that add a pleasantly bitter contrast to all kinds of salads.

• SERVES 4 •

4 heads Belgian endive, cut into 2-inch (5-cm) pieces

½ cup (50 g) walnuts

8 fresh figs, cut into ¼-inch (6.5-mm) slices

About ½ cup (120 ml) Walnut Dressing (recipe follows)

Lemon slices, for garnish

In a large bowl, combine the endive, walnuts, and figs.

Pour enough dressing over the salad just to moisten it and toss gently. Serve on salad plates and garnish with lemon slices.

Walnut Dressing

• MAKES ABOUT 1⅓ CUPS (330 ML) •

1 cup (240 ml) walnut oil

Juice of 3 lemons

½ teaspoon (2 g) freshly ground black pepper

Pinch kosher salt

Combine all of the ingredients in a blender and blend on low speed for 1 minute. Store any leftover dressing in an airtight container in the refrigerator for up to 5 days.

Stuffed Tomatoes

The yellow and red hues of a Menorcan sunset are echoed on the table in these timeless dishes. Opposite on the left, a Mediterranean summer classic: tomatoes stuffed with tuna, which are popular throughout Spain and are served for either lunch or dinner.

• SERVES 4 •

4 large tomatoes, stemmed

Kosher salt and freshly ground black pepper

2 tablespoons (30 ml) extra-virgin olive oil

½ medium yellow onion, minced

2 cloves garlic, minced

⅓ cup (80 g) pitted green olives, coarsely chopped

3 tablespoons (45 g) capers, rinsed, drained, and chopped

2 celery ribs, thinly sliced on the diagonal

One 12-ounce (340-g) can or jar of oil-packed tuna, drained and flaked

Juice of ½ lemon

2 tablespoons chopped basil, for garnish

Halve the tomatoes crosswise. Place a sieve over a bowl. Seed the tomatoes, dropping the seeds into the sieve. Press the seeds with the back of a wooden spoon to extract the juice. Discard the seeds. Hollow out the tomatoes, coarsely chopping any large pieces of tomato flesh and adding them to the bowl with the juice. Season the insides of the hollowed-out tomatoes with salt and pepper and set aside.

Heat the olive oil in a medium skillet over medium heat. When the oil is hot, add the onion and garlic and sauté until softened, about 8 minutes. Add the olives, capers, celery, and reserved tomato juice and flesh. Adjust the heat to a brisk simmer and cook until thickened, 3 to 5 minutes. Transfer to a bowl and cool until just warm.

Once the mixture has cooled slightly, add the tuna and lemon juice and season with salt and pepper. Toss to combine. Stuff the tuna mixture into the tomato halves and garnish with the basil. Serve at room temperature.

Tortilla Española

On page 154, on the right, is the pride of Spain, a classic tortilla with potatoes and onions.

• SERVES 6 •

About 1 cup (240 ml) extra-virgin olive oil

2 large white onions, cut into ¼-inch (6.5-mm) slices

1 pound (455 g) Yukon gold potatoes, peeled and cut into ¼-inch (6.5-mm) slices

Kosher salt and freshly ground black pepper

7 large eggs

Heat ¾ cup (180 ml) of the oil in a large skillet over medium-high heat. Once hot, add the onions and cook, stirring occasionally, until the onions are soft. Cover and cook for 10 additional minutes. Add the potato slices and stir to combine. The potatoes and onions should be submerged in the oil. If not, add oil to cover. Season with salt and pepper. Reduce the heat to medium-low and cook, covered, stirring occasionally, until the potatoes are almost tender but still firm in the center, about 30 minutes. Do not allow the potatoes and onions to brown. Cool slightly.

In a bowl, beat the eggs with a fork, then stir in the potatoes and onions. Toss to coat.

Heat the remaining ¼ cup (60 ml) oil in the skillet and add the egg mixture. Press down with the back of a wooden spoon to make it flat and even. Cook, covered, over low heat until the top is almost set and the underside is golden, 12 to 15 minutes. Remove from the heat and let stand, covered, for 15 minutes.

Run a silicone spatula around the tortilla and shake the skillet to loosen. Slide the tortilla out of the skillet onto a large flat plate, then overturn the skillet on top of the tortilla and invert the plate and the pan so the tortilla falls back into the skillet. Remove the plate. Cook over low heat, uncovered, until completely set, about 15 additional minutes. Slide the tortilla onto a serving plate and cut into wedges. Serve warm or at room temperature.

Grilled Sardines

Grilled sardines (opposite, top) are an easy-to-prepare appetizer. Oily fish like sardines remain moist, especially when their skin is left intact.

• SERVES 4 •

20 medium fresh sardines, cleaned and gutted

Extra-virgin olive oil, for drizzling

Kosher salt

Lemon wedges, for serving

Soak 4 bamboo skewers in water for at least 20 minutes. Rinse the sardines, pat dry, and place on a baking sheet. Drizzle olive oil over the sardines and season with salt. Thread 5 sardines on each skewer.

Heat a grill, preferably with wood chips. Grill the sardines until the skin is charred and the flesh is opaque, 1 to 2 minutes per side. Serve hot with lemon wedges.

Whole roasted garlic makes a wonderful accompaniment.

Grilled Shrimp

In Spain, it is traditional to grill shrimp (opposite, bottom) with their shells intact and then peel them by hand, but you may want to peel and devein the shrimp before you thread them on the skewers, especially if you're serving them at an elegant occasion. Either way, they are wonderfully juicy and full of flavor.

• SERVES 4 •

20 medium shrimp

Extra-virgin olive oil, for drizzling

Kosher salt

Lemon wedges for serving

Soak 4 bamboo skewers in water for at least 20 minutes. Rinse the shrimp and pat dry. Place the shrimp on a baking sheet. Drizzle olive oil over the shrimp and season with salt. Thread 5 shrimp on each skewer.

Heat a grill, preferably with wood chips. Grill the shrimp until they are pink and opaque, about 3 minutes per side. Serve hot with lemon wedges.

The Gift of Chocolate

Christopher Columbus may have been the first European to encounter the cacao plant when he saw it in Maribel's native Honduras, but he was not aware that it was used to prepare a beverage. That knowledge arrived in Spain in the sixteenth century.

In his memoir, Bernal Díaz del Castillo, one of Hernán Cortés's officers, recounts that Cortés was served the chocolate drink in 1519: "They brought him, in some fine golden cups, a certain drink made from pure cacao; they said it was for going to have relations with his women, and we paid no attention to it at that time; but what I did see was that they brought more than fifty large pitchers of good cacao with its froth and he drank of that, and the women served this drink to him with great respect."

During those years, Cortés used the Cistercian Friar Jerónimo de Aguilar as a translator. It is said that the Cistercian, in 1524 sent to Spain for the first time the recipe for the chocolate drink that soon spread through the monastic community and beyond. Others believe that the Dominican Friar Bartolomé de las Casas should be credited for the popularity of the drink, since in 1544 he accompanied a delegation of Kekchi leaders to the court of the future King Philip II of Spain, bringing gifts including cocoa beans and chocolate for drinking. Soon after, Spain began importing cacao from Mesoamerica; and, as Maribel says, "The rest is chocolate history."

Opposite: Ingredients and implements for making hot chocolate.

A SUNSET SUPPER

―――――――

The property is surrounded by a wall constructed of local stone without mortar, a characteristic architectural building style of Menorca's Talaiotic period that dates back to the end of the second millennium BCE. In this wonderful Menorcan home, the garden is the perfect spot for a late summer dinner party.

―――――――――――――――――――

Opposite: Sunset streams over a romantic dinner table, set with a joyful blue and white tablecloth, as friends gather for a Menorcan feast. Spit-roasted suckling pig is the highlight of this rustic meal, which creates a playful contrast with the crisp white chairs and the oversized traditionally designed candelabras.

Caramelized Figs

Figs are mentioned in Sumerian stone tablets dating back to 2500 BCE, making them one of the fruits humans have been consuming longest. These figs work well as a dessert, but they also make an unusual accompaniment to meat dishes.

• SERVES 8 •

16 fresh figs

½ cup (100 g) turbinado sugar

1 stick (8 tablespoons/113 g) salted butter, at room temperature, cut into cubes

Green grapes, for garnish

In a skillet large enough to hold the figs in a single layer, combine ½ cup (120 ml) water and the sugar. Place the whole figs in the liquid stem-side up. Cover and bring to a boil over medium heat.

Turn the heat to low and cook until the figs are caramelized, 5 to 7 minutes. Scatter on the butter and when it has melted, remove the pan from the heat.

Remove the figs and place in a shallow serving bowl. Reduce the caramel with the butter a little and pour it over the figs. Allow to cool to room temperature before serving. Garnish with the grapes.

Flourless Orange-Almond Cake
with Chocolate Topping

This scrumptious orange-almond cake topped with chocolate beautifully combines three of my favorite flavors. Fluffy and moist, it makes an elegant dessert.

• SERVES 8 •

Unsalted butter, for the pan

1½ cups (150 g) almond flour

1 teaspoon (5 g) baking powder

Pinch kosher salt

4 large eggs, at room temperature, separated

½ cup (100 g) sugar

Grated zest of 1 large orange

8 ounces (225 g) 64% dark chocolate, chopped

Cocoa powder, for dusting

Preheat the oven to 350°F/175°C. Butter an 8- or 9-inch (20- or 23-cm) round springform pan and line the bottom with a parchment paper disk.

In a medium bowl, combine the almond flour, baking powder, and salt.

With a stand or handheld mixer, beat the egg whites on medium speed until light and foamy, about 1 minute. With the machine running, gradually add ¼ cup (50 g) of the sugar. Increase the speed to medium-high and beat until the egg whites form soft peaks, 1 to 2 additional minutes.

Combine the egg yolks, orange zest, and remaining ¼ cup (50 g) sugar and beat with a wooden spoon until smooth. Stir in the almond flour mixture and beat until smooth. (The mixture will be quite thick.)

Add about one-third of the egg white mixture and stir it in. Gently fold in the remaining egg whites with a rubber spatula, taking care not to deflate the batter too much. Scrape the batter into the prepared pan and bake until it is puffed and a tester inserted in the center comes out with just a few crumbs, about 30 minutes. Remove to a rack to cool completely. To unmold, run a knife around the edge of the pan to loosen the cake, then unbuckle and remove the ring.

To make the chocolate topping, melt the chopped chocolate in a double boiler (or a heatproof bowl set over a pot of simmering water) over low heat. Spread in a thick layer on a baking sheet and refrigerate until it begins to set but is not yet solid, about 30 minutes.

Once it is almost set, cut out irregularly sized strips of chocolate. Arrange the strips to cover the surface of the cake, overlapping in parts for a rustic effect. Dust with cocoa powder and serve.

Above, left to right: A long table in the garden set for a relaxed dinner;
Menorca's rugged coastline; spit-roasted suckling pig.

DINING WITH LEGENDS

Cadaqués is a town on Spain's eastern Costa Brava. Its history goes back thousands of years. Among its most defining chapters are the cultural impact of the Greeks and Romans, and the incursions by buccaneers and pirates in the fifteenth and sixteenth centuries. In the twentieth century, this charming *pueblo blanco*, located on the Cap de Creus, became a cultural beacon when Dalí made his home there, attracting artists such as Picasso, Magritte, and Duchamp.

Opposite: *Inside a Cadaqués home, guests start dinner with a cocktail and laughter. This evening's selection includes Kiwi Caipiroska and Strawberry Gin Smash.*

Clams
with Garlic & Wine

Adding to the rural feel of this appetizer, the sautéed clams are served in small dual-handled serving pans. I love finding new uses for all kinds of kitchen items. Don't be afraid to play around—entertaining should be fun.

• SERVES 6 TO 8 •

6 tablespoons (90 g) salted butter

1 tablespoon (10 g) minced garlic

1 cup (240 ml) white wine

3 pounds (1.5 kg) small clams, such as littleneck clams, purged and scrubbed

2 tablespoons (30 ml) freshly squeezed lemon juice

1 tablespoon (2 g) chopped flat-leaf parsley, optional

1 tablespoon (2 g) chopped fresh dill, optional

In a large skillet, melt 3 tablespoons (45 g) of the butter. Add the garlic and cook just until fragrant, 30 to 40 seconds. Add the wine and bring to a boil.

Add the clams, the lemon juice, and the remaining 3 tablespoons (45 g) butter. Cover the pan with a lid and steam for 8 minutes. Remove the pan from the heat and remove and discard any unopened clams. Sprinkle on the parsley and dill, if using. Serve directly from the pan or transfer to smaller serving dishes.

Coca de Vidre
Glass Flatbread

This sweet flatbread is meant to be thin and crisp enough to shatter like glass—the *vidre* of its name—as shown here. However, the recipe for this Catalan specialty makes a slightly puffy flatbread. Both versions are topped with pine nuts for extra crunch.

• SERVES 4 •

3 cups (375 g) all-purpose flour, plus more for sprinkling

1 teaspoon (5 g) kosher salt

2 tablespoons (20 g) active dry yeast

1 tablespoon (12 g) sugar or 1 tablespoon (20 g) honey

2 tablespoons (30 ml) extra-virgin olive oil, plus more for the pan

Pine nuts, for sprinkling

In a large bowl, combine the 3 cups (375 g) flour and salt with a wooden spoon.

Pour 1½ cups (360 ml) warm water into a small bowl and whisk in the yeast and sugar. Set aside until the yeast blooms, 5 to 7 minutes. Stir in the 2 tablespoons (30 ml) olive oil.

Add the yeast mixture to the flour mixture and stir until the dough comes together. (You can also use a stand mixer fitted with the dough hook.) The dough should be a bit wet. Add a little water if it seems dry and crumbly.

Cover the bowl and set aside in a warm place until doubled in size, 2 to 3 hours.

Brush an 8- or 9-inch (20- or 23-cm) round or rectangular baking pan with oil and turn the dough into the pan. Sprinkle the top of the dough with a light coating of flour so that the dough does not stick to your hands. With your fingertips, press and stretch the dough to fit the pan. Allow to rest for another 30 minutes.

Meanwhile, preheat the oven to 450°F/230°C. Sprinkle pine nuts on top of the dough and bake until crisp and golden, 30 to 35 minutes. Serve warm.

Crema Catalana
con Ananas

I like to make this Spanish custard with milk, rather than cream, for a lighter and more delicate result. The pineapple rings in the bottom are a fun surprise for guests. Crema catalana looks wonderful in a terra-cotta dish, as shown here, but will taste just as good in a white porcelain ramekin.

• SERVES 6 •

3 tablespoons (45 g) unsalted butter

Six ½-inch (1.25-cm) pineapple rings

Kosher salt

2 tablespoons (16 g) confectioners' sugar

3 cups (720 ml) whole milk

1 strip lemon zest

1 strip orange zest

1 cinnamon stick

6 large egg yolks

½ cup plus 3 tablespoons (140 g) granulated sugar

2 tablespoons plus 1½ teaspoons (20 g) cornstarch

Melt 1½ tablespoons (22.5 g) of the butter in a large nonstick skillet over medium-low heat. Add 3 of the pineapple rings and a pinch of salt. Cook, turning once, until lightly browned on each side, 1 to 2 minutes per side.

Sprinkle the tops with 1 tablespoon (8 g) of the confectioners' sugar and flip the rings. Cook until caramelized on the bottom, about 1 minute. Remove to a plate and repeat with the remaining butter, pineapple, salt, and confectioners' sugar.

Place 1 pineapple ring each in the bottom of each of six 8-ounce (240 ml) ovenproof serving dishes or ramekins.

Combine the milk, lemon zest, orange zest, and cinnamon stick in a medium saucepan. Bring to a gentle simmer over low heat and simmer for 1 minute, then remove from the heat and set aside to steep for 10 minutes.

In a heatproof bowl, whisk together the egg yolks, ½ cup (100 g) of the granulated sugar, the cornstarch, and a pinch of salt in a large bowl.

Remove the cinnamon stick and peels from the milk. Pour the warm milk mixture into the yolk mixture in a thin stream, whisking constantly. Whisk until smooth. Return the mixture to the saucepan and place over medium-low heat. Cook, stirring constantly, until a few bubbles pop to the surface and the mixture thickens enough to coat the back of a spoon, 4 to 6 minutes.

Strain into a large spouted measuring cup, then divide among the serving dishes. Refrigerate until chilled and set, at least 4 hours.

When ready to serve, sprinkle the dishes with the remaining 3 tablespoons (40 g) granulated sugar. Caramelize the surfaces with a kitchen torch (or under the broiler, keeping a close eye on them to be sure they don't scorch) and serve immediately.

- IN -

FRANCE

French cuisine is a complex tapestry of centuries-old culinary traditions enriched by wide-ranging and distinct regional influences. The cuisine of Provence, in the south, skews to seafood, vegetables, and fruits.

The French influence on Maribel's culinary style is undeniable. She explained, "My food is inspired by my Central American upbringing, but also permeated by the flavors I discovered during the many years I spent traveling with my husband, Jacques, to France, where he grew up."

MARIBEL'S MENUS

(recipes in roman are provided)

A LIGHT SUPPER IN THE SHADE
OF A GRANDE ALLÉE
Saint-Rémy-de-Provence

Côtes de Provence Rosé
Roasted Asparagus with Chopped Egg . . . 182
Smoked Salmon with Lemon Wedges and Basil
Prosciutto, Dried Apricots, Figs, Prunes & Currants
Caprese Salad with Currants, Strawberries & Tomatoes . . . 182
Green Salad
Fruit Salad

DINNER IN PROVENCE
Saint-Rémy-de-Provence

Côtes du Rhone
Jacques's Short Ribs with Chocolate Sauce . . . 190
Provençal Ratatouille Tian . . . 193
Melted Dark Chocolate for Dipping (served with figs)

A FEAST OF MANY COLORS
Saint-Rémy-de-Provence

Tavel Rosé
Potatoes with Herb Butter . . . 196
Stuffed Artichokes . . . 197
Baby Zucchini with Toasted Pine Nuts
Tomatoes with Niçoise Olives & Basil
Butter Lettuce with Sliced Figs
Endives, Roquefort & Apples
Orange Beignets with Powdered Sugar . . . 199

*Opposite: The sun sets on yet another perfect day in Provence. **Following pages, clockwise from left:** A long table was arranged in the shade of a row of plane trees; a classically designed pavilion; the interior of a typical French bistro; the age-old majesty of Mediterranean pines; the exterior of the Bistrot de Saint Rémy in Provence.*

A LIGHT SUPPER IN THE SHADE OF A GRAND ALLÉE

Something extraordinary happens when the magic of nature intersects with hospitality and generosity. In Provence, the region's beauty and an unmistakable *joie de vivre* reign above all, enchanting our senses and enthralling the visitor with this unique identity. In this magical garden in bloom, lavender, rosemary, and oregano infuse the air with the unmistakable scents of a very French Garden of Eden.

Opposite: Potted olive and herb centerpieces and rosé wine bring the joy of summer to the table and perfume the air.

Roasted Asparagus
with Chopped Egg

The *Old Farmer's Almanac* tells us that asparagus can grow in most temperate regions of the world but does best in cooler areas with long winters. The stalks and spears of the many varieties of asparagus are the only edible parts; they pop out of the earth in spring.

• SERVES 4 •

3 tablespoons (45 ml) extra-virgin olive oil

1 teaspoon (5 ml) freshly squeezed lemon juice

Kosher salt and freshly ground black pepper

4 hard-boiled eggs, peeled and roughly chopped

2 tablespoons (30 g) unsalted butter

8 large green asparagus spears, stalks peeled and trimmed

Smoked paprika (pimentón), to taste

Prepare the vinaigrette by whisking together the oil and lemon juice in a small bowl. Season with salt and pepper and set aside.

Place the chopped eggs in a medium bowl and lightly season with salt and pepper. Drizzle on about 2 tablespoons (30 ml) of the vinaigrette and gently toss to coat. Set aside.

Heat a large skillet over medium-high heat and add the butter. Once melted, add the asparagus in a single layer and cook until crisp-tender, about 4 minutes. Season with a pinch of salt and pepper and add the smoked paprika, if using.

Remove the asparagus from the heat and arrange on a serving platter. Spoon the remaining vinaigrette over the asparagus and top with the eggs. Serve warm.

Caprese Salad
with Currants, Strawberries & Tomatoes

Currants are a type of Ribes berry and come in a variety of colors, including black, red, and white. Their distinctive tart flavor adds a welcome punch to this classic summer dish.

• SERVES 4 •

1 heirloom beefsteak tomato, cut into thin wedges

1 ball mozzarella, cut into ¼-inch (6.5-mm) slices

20 basil leaves

4 ounces (115 g) thinly sliced prosciutto crudo or Serrano ham, optional

5 strawberries, hulled and halved

4 small clusters red currants

1 cluster black currants, stemmed and sliced

2 tablespoons (30 ml) extra-virgin olive oil

Kosher salt and freshly ground black pepper

Arrange the tomato and mozzarella slices and the basil leaves in a pinwheel on a platter. Place the prosciutto, if using, in the middle. Scatter the strawberries on top. Garnish with the red currant clusters and a scattering of sliced black currants.

Drizzle with the olive oil and season with salt and pepper to taste.

Above, left to right: *A formal table set al fresco; Caprese Salad with Currants, Strawberries & Tomatoes (page 182); local vineyards at sunset; figs prepared for dipping in Maribel's chocolate sauce (page 124).*

French at Heart

French cuisine holds a treasure trove of flavors that Maribel has embraced after spending many summers in France with her husband Jacques and their daughter.

This culinary tradition evolved from simple, but delicious, locally sourced dishes to a *haute cuisine*, with its highly refined dishes. "French" became synonymous with fine dining; a culinary style now known as *classique*.

In the 1960s and '70s, French *nouvelle cuisine* embraced lighter dishes and flavors, blending old and new, regional, and global flavors—in some way, returning to its roots. Most recently, French restaurateurs responded to their clients demands with *bistronomy*, a cuisine that favors simple, local, and seasonal dishes prepared using gastronomic cooking methods. This is the cuisine that inspires Maribel's culinary style (albeit with a Latino twist).

From her reliance on using the freshest local ingredients and respect for seasonal rhythms to the decor of her home, her fashion style, and the choice of the name MarieBelle for her chocolate company, this world traveler and native Honduran seems most definitely French at heart.

Opposite: Coffee and chocolate are a classic pairing. Here, a selection of MarieBelle's chocolate ganaches are decorated with Jacques Lieberman's abstract painting motifs, while others portray chic New Yorkers sitting in the lotus position, gathering with friends, and even enjoying a day at the beach.

DINNER IN PROVENCE

The days of summer in Provence are filled with
joyful banter; long, lazy lunches; and walks in the
shade of its majestic pines. From Roman ruins to
ancient olive groves and weathered farmhouses,
the sights and sounds of Provence seem to exist
outside of time, in a world of their own.

***Opposite:** A romantic French garden setting provides the
perfect frame for the dining table set with a blue-and-
white tablecloth, matching napkins, and floral-patterned
dishware. The hand-blown purple glasses provide a pop
of contrasting color. The dinner ends with figs paired with
a chocolate dipping sauce served in a fondue pot, pictured
on page 185.*

Jacques's Short Ribs
with Chocolate Sauce

Short ribs have a rich culinary history on the European continent, particularly in France and Italy. This cut comes from the chuck, plate, rib, or brisket section of a cow. My husband, Jacques, was a master of short ribs.

• SERVES 6 •

6 bone-in beef short ribs (about 10 to 12 ounces/280 to 340 g each)

Kosher salt and freshly ground black pepper

All-purpose flour, for dredging

¼ cup plus 2 tablespoons (90 ml) extra-virgin olive oil

6 ribs celery, chopped

4 medium carrots, chopped

2 medium yellow onions, chopped

3 cloves garlic, crushed and peeled

1 bottle plus ½ cup (870 ml) good-quality Burgundy wine

1 cup (240 ml) unsalted beef broth

1 cup (240 ml) unsalted chicken broth

1 tablespoon (15 g) tomato paste

3 bay leaves

3 sprigs thyme, optional

2 large bulbs fennel, trimmed, cored, and cut into wedges

2 tablespoons (30 g) unsalted butter, at room temperature

1 tablespoon (5 g) unsweetened cocoa powder

2 sprigs rosemary, for garnish

Season the short ribs all over with salt and pepper. Spread some flour in a shallow bowl. Heat a large skillet over medium-high heat and add 2 tablespoons (30 ml) of the olive oil. Once the oil is hot, dredge the short ribs in flour, tapping off the excess, and add to the skillet. Brown on all sides, 4 to 5 minutes altogether. With tongs, remove the short ribs to a large plate.

Add the celery to the skillet and cook until it begins to soften, about 5 minutes. With a slotted spoon, remove to the plate with the short ribs. Add 2 more tablespoons (30 ml) of the olive oil to the skillet. Add the carrots and cook until browned, about 5 minutes. With a slotted spoon remove to the plate.

Add the remaining 2 tablespoons (30 ml) of the olive oil along with the onions and garlic. Cook until the onions begin to wilt, about 5 minutes. With a slotted spoon remove to the plate.

In a large Dutch oven, combine the vegetables, the bottle (750 ml) of wine, beef broth, chicken broth, tomato paste, bay leaves, and thyme, if using. Season with salt and pepper. Bring to a simmer and nestle the short ribs in the liquid. Cover and simmer, stirring occasionally, over low heat until the short ribs are tender and falling off the bone, about 2 hours.

Remove the short ribs to a platter and cover to keep warm. Strain the cooking liquid into a bowl and return it to the Dutch oven. Bring to a rapid simmer over medium heat and add the fennel. Simmer until the fennel is tender and translucent, 15 to 20 minutes. Strain into a bowl and reserve the cooking liquid. Arrange the fennel around the short ribs on the platter.

Bring the remaining ½ cup (120 ml) wine to a boil in a medium saucepan over medium-high heat. Boil until reduced by half. Add the strained cooking liquid and boil until slightly thickened, 1 to 2 minutes. Whisk in the butter. Whisk in the cocoa powder until smooth. Garnish the ribs and fennel with rosemary and serve the sauce on the side.

Provençal Ratatouille Tian

A ratatouille tian, also known as a tian Provençal, uses the same ingredients as traditional French ratatouille. However, the vegetables are sliced (not diced), layered (not tossed together), and baked (not sautéed). A white oval stoneware gratin dish is the perfect choice for both cooking and serving the tian.

• SERVES 8 •

SAUCE

1 medium tomato, chopped

1 small Spanish onion, chopped

½ green bell pepper, seeded and chopped

½ jalapeño pepper, seeded

¼ bunch cilantro sprigs

¼ cup (60 ml) extra-virgin olive oil

One 28-ounce (800-g) can crushed tomatoes

1 teaspoon (5 g) kosher salt, plus more to taste

Freshly ground black pepper

¼ cup (10 g) torn basil leaves

VEGETABLES

2 small Italian eggplant

4 ripe plum tomatoes

2 zucchini

2 yellow squash

⅓ cup (75 ml) extra-virgin olive oil

2 cloves garlic, minced

2 tablespoons (12 g) chopped fresh basil leaves

2 teaspoons (4 g) chopped fresh thyme leaves, plus thyme sprigs for garnish

1 teaspoon (5 g) kosher salt

Freshly ground black pepper

Preheat the oven to 400°F/205°C.

For the sauce, combine the tomato, onion, green pepper, jalapeño, and cilantro in a blender and blend until smooth.

Heat the olive oil in a medium Dutch oven over medium heat. When the oil is hot, add the puree and bring to a simmer. Cook, stirring occasionally, until slightly reduced and concentrated, 3 to 4 minutes. Add the crushed tomatoes and season with the 1 teaspoon (5 g) salt and a generous amount of pepper. Simmer until very thick and flavorful, about 20 minutes. Stir in the shredded basil. Taste and adjust seasoning.

Meanwhile, use a mandoline to thinly slice the eggplant, tomatoes, zucchini, and squash crosswise on a bias. Put the vegetables in a large bowl and drizzle with the olive oil. Toss to coat in the oil. Sprinkle with the garlic, basil, thyme, salt, and pepper and toss once more.

Spread a 1-inch (2.5-cm) layer of sauce in a 15 by 10-inch (38 by 25-cm) or larger oval gratin dish, reserving the rest of the sauce. Starting from the outer edge of the dish, arrange alternating slices of the vegetables in concentric rings on top of the sauce. (Fit the vegetables as snugly and neatly as you can.)

Cover the gratin dish tightly with foil and bake until the mixture is bubbly around the edges, 45 to 50 minutes. Uncover and bake until the vegetables are tender and browned, 15 to 20 additional minutes. Garnish with thyme sprigs and serve with the reserved sauce on the side.

A FEAST OF MANY COLORS

Fresh produce is the star of any Provençal meal. This extraordinarily beautiful and historic region of France is blessed with mild weather, sunshine, and rivers and streams, making it suitable for a variety of crops—from lavender fields that grow on its plateaus and strawberries and fruit trees in the plains to the iconic vines and olive trees that flourish everywhere.

Opposite: Tomatoes, baby zucchini, a salad with figs, endive with Roquefort and apples, and Stuffed Artichokes (page 197) form a colorful buffet that blends beautifully with the native flowers of this charmed garden.

Potatoes
with Herb Butter

The humble potato comes in numerous varieties. All are a great source of energy. Steamed potatoes with parsley are a beloved staple throughout France.

• SERVES 6 •

3 pounds (1.5 kg) Yukon Gold potatoes, peeled and thickly sliced

1 stick (8 tablespoons/113 g) unsalted butter

1 tablespoon (3 g) coarsely chopped flat-leaf parsley leaves

1 teaspoon (1 g) finely chopped dill fronds

1 teaspoon (1 g) finely chopped tarragon leaves

1 teaspoon (4 g) grated lemon zest

½ teaspoon (2.5 g) kosher salt

¼ teaspoon (1 g) freshly ground black pepper

Set a large 6-quart (6-l) stockpot on the stove and place a steamer basket in the bottom of the pot. Fill the pot with 1 inch (2.5 cm) water.

Place the potatoes in the steamer basket. Cover the pot and turn the heat to medium-high. Steam the potatoes until tender, 15 to 20 minutes.

In a medium saucepan, melt the butter over medium heat. Mix in the parsley, dill, tarragon, and lemon zest. Add the salt and pepper and stir to combine.

Transfer the cooked potatoes to a large serving bowl. Drizzle with the herb butter. Gently stir with a wooden spoon to coat. Serve warm.

Stuffed Artichokes

Native to the Mediterranean, the artichoke is a versatile vegetable that can be steamed, grilled, sautéed, or stuffed. Stuffed artichokes make an impressive vegetarian appetizer or side dish for a dinner party. This recipe can easily be doubled to serve a crowd.

• SERVES 6 •

¼ cup (60 ml) freshly squeezed lemon juice

6 small artichokes

1 cup (100 g) Italian-seasoned breadcrumbs or panko

½ cup (50 g) grated Pecorino Romano

½ cup (50 g) grated Parmigiano Reggiano

8 cloves garlic, minced

1 cup (240 ml) extra-virgin olive oil, plus more for brushing

Place the lemon juice in a large pot of water. Peel off the rough outer leaves of the artichokes and peel the stems. Trim off the tops and bottoms, making flat bases, and snip off any sharp points with kitchen shears. (Reserve any stem pieces.) Scoop out the fuzzy chokes. As you finish trimming them, drop them in the pot of water. Cover, bring to a boil, and boil until tender, 30 to 40 minutes. Check by pulling an outer leaf. If it pulls away easily, the artichokes are ready. Drain the artichokes and allow to cool.

Preheat the oven to 325°F/165°C.

In a medium bowl, combine the breadcrumbs, cheeses, and garlic. With a wooden spoon, stir in ½ cup (120 ml) of the oil, and mix well to combine.

Brush a large baking dish with oil and arrange the cooled artichokes in it, standing on their flat bases. Scatter in any reserved stem pieces. With a spoon, stuff the artichokes with the breadcrumb mixture. Drizzle the remaining ½ cup (120 ml) oil over the top of the stuffed artichokes.

Pour 2 cups (480 l) of water down the side of the baking dish. Cover the dish with aluminum foil and bake for 45 minutes.

Remove the foil, turn the oven to broil, and broil the artichokes on the lowest rack of the oven until crisp, 10 to 15 minutes. Serve hot.

Orange Beignets
with Powdered Sugar

Beignets are one of the most beloved simple and not-too-sweet dishes in France. (Others include crêpes, like the ones on page 84, and gauffres, or waffles.) Citrus elevates these to an extra-special treat.

• MAKES 16 BEIGNETS •

2 cups (250 g) all-purpose flour, plus more for the work surface

2 tablespoons (20 g) active dry yeast

3 tablespoons (45 ml) freshly squeezed orange juice

1 cup (240 ml) warm whole milk

1 large egg

2 tablespoons (25 g) granulated sugar

1 teaspoon (5 ml) pure vanilla extract

1 teaspoon (4 g) grated lemon zest

1½ tablespoons (20 g) unsalted butter, softened to room temperature

About 2 cups (480 ml) vegetable oil for frying

Confectioners' sugar, for serving

Melted Dark Chocolate for Dipping (see page 124), for serving

Sift the 2 cups (250 g) flour into a large bowl. Create a well in the middle of the flour and add the yeast, orange juice, milk, egg, granulated sugar, vanilla, lemon zest, and butter. Mix to combine thoroughly, then knead until smooth. Return to the bowl and cover with cheesecloth. Let rise in a cool, dry place for 1 hour.

On a lightly floured work surface, roll the dough into a square about ⅛ inch (3 mm) thick. Cut the dough into 2 by 2-inch (5 by 5-cm) squares.

Line a large plate or serving platter with paper towels.

Add enough of the vegetable oil to come up the sides of a heavy skillet and place over medium heat. Bring to 325°F/165°C. Using a slotted spoon or skimmer, lower 2 or 3 squares into the oil, making sure they don't stick together. Fry until golden on one side, 1 to 2 minutes. Flip, then fry on the other side for 1 additional minute. Transfer to the prepared plate. Continue with the remaining dough, adding more oil as necessary.

Sprinkle with confectioners' sugar and serve piping hot with chocolate for dipping.

Note: How far into the chocolate to dip the beignet is a hotly debated topic, and ultimately a highly personal decision. The answer is to experiment.

- IN -

ITALY

While Spain is intrinsically linked to Maribel's native Honduras, France is where her heart resides and New York is her home, but Maribel's fascination with the old, the new, and the eclectic has led her to Northern Italy again and again.

This is a region of Italy rich in complexity, where the horizon is defined by both the shores of the Adriatic Sea and the base of the Alpine mountains; a world that reflects the importance of its agricultural lands as well as the historical connection to its transalpine neighbors.

Maribel is particularly drawn to Northern Italy's distinct culinary flavors, known for its rich sauces, fragrant cheeses, slow-cooked meats, and satisfying polenta dishes.

MARIBEL'S MENUS

(recipes in roman are provided)

THE TIME TRAVELER
Alessandria, Piemonte

Polenta with Cocoa Powder . . . 208

A TABLE WITH A VIEW
Piemonte

Roero Arneis
Supplì . . . 212
Parmigiano Reggiano, Taleggio & Gorgonzola Cheeses
Hazelnuts
Polenta al Forno . . . 215
Green Salad
Osso Buco . . . 216
Buttered Peas

DINING BY THE LAKE
Villa di Laglio, Lake Como

Favorita or Langhe Rosato
Piemonte Biova Bread
Green Salad
Veal Meatballs with Lemon Sauce . . . 222

ON THE SANTA MARGHERITA SHORE
Santa Margherita, Liguria

Grapefruit Cocktail . . . 228
Insalata Nizzarda . . . 228
Focaccia with Ricotta & Prosciutto Cotto . . . 231
Focaccia with Walnuts, Figs & Honey . . . 231
Molten Chocolate Cakes

Opposite: Small farms dot the rolling hills of the valley below Castelnuovo Scrivia in the Piemonte region, which produces some of Italy's best wine and food. **Following page, clockwise from left:** *The port of Santa Margherita; a candlelight dinner in the rolling hills of the Po Valley; the Sanctuary of the Madonna of the Letter in Santa Margherita; a bathing establishment on Santa Margherita's beachfront; the courtyard of Castello di Montegioco.*

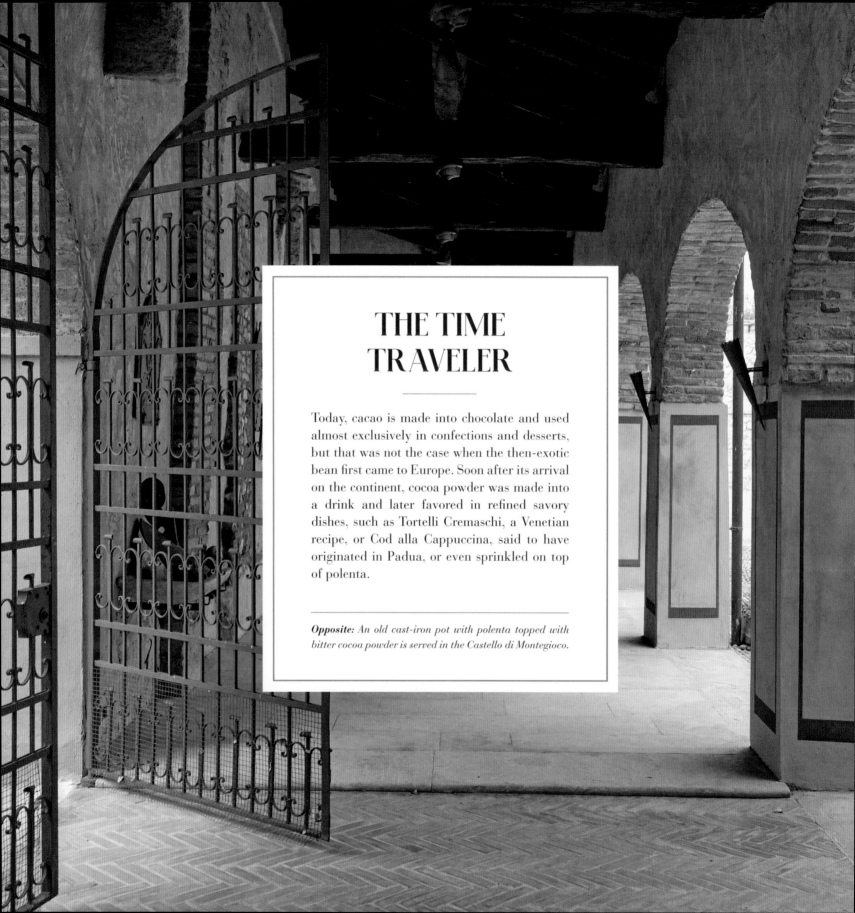

THE TIME TRAVELER

Today, cacao is made into chocolate and used almost exclusively in confections and desserts, but that was not the case when the then-exotic bean first came to Europe. Soon after its arrival on the continent, cocoa powder was made into a drink and later favored in refined savory dishes, such as Tortelli Cremaschi, a Venetian recipe, or Cod alla Cappuccina, said to have originated in Padua, or even sprinkled on top of polenta.

Opposite: An old cast-iron pot with polenta topped with bitter cocoa powder is served in the Castello di Montegioco.

Polenta
with Cocoa Powder

When the winds and the rain whip around the streets of Milan or the canals of Venice, when snow blows among the alpine peaks in Cortina and bone-chilling cold envelops the north, polenta—a centuries-old and much-loved comfort food—is the answer.

• SERVES 6 •

1 teaspoon (5 g) kosher salt

1 cup (155 g) polenta (not instant)

3 tablespoons (45 g) unsalted butter, cut into pieces

¼ cup (25 g) grated Parmigiano Reggiano

1 tablespoon (7.5 g) cocoa powder

Place 4 cups (960 ml) water in a large saucepan with the salt and bring to a boil. Once the water is boiling, gradually add the polenta in a thin stream while whisking. Whisk until smooth. Adjust the heat so the polenta is barely simmering and cook, stirring frequently, until the mixture is thick, the polenta no longer tastes raw, and the individual grains of polenta are tender, 45 to 50 minutes. Don't hurry this process.

When the polenta is fully cooked, turn off the heat. Stir in the butter and the Parmigiano.

Spoon the hot polenta into individual serving bowls. Sprinkle with cocoa powder and serve.

A TABLE
WITH A VIEW

The Italian countryside is the setting of count-less romantic narratives, and it inspired literary masters such as Percy Bysshe Shelley, who wrote:

As the sunrise to the night,
As the north wind to the clouds,
As the earthquake's fiery flight,
Ruining mountain solitudes,
Everlasting Italy,
Be those hopes and fears on thee.

Opposite: *Evening light casts magic over the idyllic setting for a rural aperitivo.*

Supplì

Italy boasts two kinds of traditional rice croquettes—Roman *supplì* (shown opposite right) and Sicilian arancini. *Supplì* are cylinders made with tomato sauce and mozzarella, while for arancini the rice is tossed with a meat-based ragù of beef and peas and shaped into spheres or pyramids.

• MAKES 16 CROQUETTES, SERVES 4 TO 6 •

3 cups (720 ml) chicken broth

1 cup (240 ml) tomato puree

12 saffron threads

2 tablespoons (30 ml) extra-virgin olive oil

2 medium shallots, minced

1¼ cups (230 g) arborio rice

1 cup (240 ml) dry white wine

Kosher salt and freshly ground black pepper

1 cup (100 g) grated Parmigiano Reggiano

20 basil leaves, finely chopped

½ cup (115 g) diced mozzarella

All-purpose flour, for dredging

2 large eggs

2 cups (200 g) fine dry breadcrumbs

Vegetable oil, for frying

Combine the chicken broth, tomato puree, and saffron in a medium saucepan over low heat and bring to a low simmer.

Meanwhile, heat the olive oil over medium heat in a medium saucepan. Add the shallots and cook until translucent, 2 to 3 minutes. Add the rice and stir to combine. Pour in the wine and adjust the heat to a simmer. Cook, stirring, until most of the wine has been absorbed, 1 to 2 minutes. Ladle in enough of the broth mixture just to cover the rice. Simmer, stirring often, until most of the liquid has been absorbed. Continue cooking and adding the broth mixture in small amounts until the rice is tender but still a bit al dente, 15 to 18 minutes total. (You may not need all of the liquid.) Season with salt and pepper.

Remove from the heat and stir in the grated Parmigiano and half of the basil. Spread on a baking sheet and allow to cool completely.

Portion the cooled rice into 16 equal golf ball–size mounds. Roll into balls. Make an indentation in each and fill with some of the mozzarella, then close the indentation, encasing the mozzarella in rice. Form the balls into oblong cylinders.

Spread some flour in a shallow bowl. Beat the eggs with a pinch of salt in a second shallow bowl. Combine the breadcrumbs and remaining chopped basil in a third shallow bowl. Heat about 2 inches (5 cm) of oil in a medium Dutch oven to 350°F/175°C. Line a large plate or baking sheet with paper towels.

Dredge the cylinders in the flour, eggs, then breadcrumbs, coating them evenly and completely.

Fry, working in batches to avoid crowding, until deep golden brown, about 4 minutes. Let the oil return to 350°F/175°C between batches. Drain on paper towels. Season lightly with salt.

Serve hot with marinara for dipping, if desired.

Polenta al Forno

Cooked polenta that has cooled and set can be sliced and crisped to add another textural dimension.

• SERVES 6 •

Extra-virgin olive oil, for brushing and pan-frying

1½ teaspoons (7 g) kosher salt, plus more to taste

1 cup (155 g) polenta (not instant)

4 tablespoons (57 g) unsalted butter, cut into pieces

¼ cup (25 g) grated Parmigiano Reggiano or cotija

¼ cup (10 g) chopped fresh chives, optional

2 tablespoons (5 g) chopped cilantro leaves, optional

Lightly brush an 11 by 7-inch (17 by 28-cm) baking dish with oil and set aside.

Place 4 cups (960 ml) water in a large saucepan with the 1½ teaspoons (7 g) salt and bring to a boil. Once the water is boiling, gradually add the polenta in a thin stream while whisking. Whisk until smooth. Adjust the heat so the polenta is barely simmering and cook, stirring frequently, until the mixture is thick, the polenta no longer tastes raw, and the individual grains of polenta are tender, 45 to 50 minutes. Don't hurry this process. Vigorously stir in the butter until combined. Remove from the heat and stir in the Parmigiano and the chives and cilantro, if using.

Spread the hot polenta in an even layer, about ¾ inch (2 cm) thick, in the prepared baking dish. Refrigerate until cold and firm, about 2 hours.

When you're ready to serve, preheat the oven to 250°F/120°C with a baking sheet on the middle rack. Line a plate with paper towels. Unmold the polenta and cut into 2 by 1-inch (5 by 2.5-cm) rectangles.

Heat a large skillet over medium-high heat and add a thin film of olive oil. When the oil is hot, add enough polenta rectangles to fit in one layer and fry, turning once, until golden brown, about 3 minutes per side. Transfer to the prepared plate to drain briefly, then keep warm on the baking sheet in the oven. Fry the remaining polenta, adding more oil to the pan as needed.

Once all of the polenta is fried, transfer to a serving platter, season with salt, and serve immediately.

Osso Buco

The literal translation of the Italian *osso buco* is "bone with a hole." The marrow in that bone remains luxuriously rich as the meat cooks. It's traditional to serve herbaceous gremolata with this satisfying dish.

• SERVES 6 •

6 bone-in crosscut pieces veal shank, about 1 inch (2.5 cm) thick, each one trussed with kitchen twine

Kosher salt and freshly ground black pepper

All-purpose flour, for dredging

3 tablespoons (45 ml) extra-virgin olive oil

1 medium yellow onion, minced

1 large carrot, minced

2 ribs celery, minced

1/3 cup (80 g) tomato paste

4 cloves garlic, minced, plus 1 whole crushed clove for the gremolata

Leaves of 1 sprig fresh rosemary, minced

Pinch crushed red pepper flakes

1 cup (240 ml) dry white wine

3 cups (720 ml) beef broth

4 fresh bay leaves

1 cup (40 g) loosely packed flat-leaf parsley leaves

Grated zest of 1 lemon

Season the meat with salt and pepper. Spread some flour in a shallow bowl. Place a Dutch oven large enough to fit all of the meat in a single snug layer over medium heat and add 2 tablespoons (30 ml) of the olive oil. Once the oil is hot, dredge half of the pieces of meat in flour, tapping off the excess, and add to the pot. Brown on both sides, about 2 minutes per side, and remove to a plate with tongs. Add the remaining 1 tablespoon (15 ml) olive oil and repeat with the remaining meat, then remove that meat to the plate with tongs.

In the Dutch oven, sauté the onion, carrot, and celery until softened, 4 to 5 minutes. Clear a spot in the middle of the pan and add the tomato paste, minced garlic, rosemary, and red pepper flakes. Cook, stirring, until the tomato paste is slightly darkened and the garlic and rosemary are fragrant, about 1 minute. Stir to combine with the vegetables.

Add the wine and bring to a boil, then reduce by half, about 1 minute. Add the chicken broth and bay leaves and return to a simmer. Nestle the meat in the pot in a single layer, adding a little water, if needed, so it is almost (but not completely) covered in liquid. Adjust the heat to a simmer, cover, and cook until the meat is tender but not falling off the bone, 1 hour 15 minutes to 1½ hours.

Transfer the meat to a cutting board and remove the twine. Fish out and discard the bay leaves. Bring the sauce to a rapid simmer and cook until it is slightly thickened and coats the back of a spoon, 3 to 4 minutes. Remove from the heat, return the meat to the pot, and cover to keep warm while you make the gremolata.

For the gremolata, mince the remaining garlic clove and the parsley together. Add the lemon zest and chop a few times to combine.

Arrange the osso buco and sauce on a platter. Pass the gremolata on the side.

Italian Excellence

A passionate Francophile, Maribel ascribes squarely to the dictum that "the French do it better," but she can never say enough good things about what Maribel calls "the four great Italian masterpieces."

First on the list is focaccia. This humblest of foods made of just flour, water, salt, and a little yeast has been around for more than 2,000 years. Every perfect bite tells a story.

Second is the treasured Piedmont (or Alba) white truffle. Among the ten most expensive foods in the world, it is the undisputed ruler of the fungus kingdom. The fact that it is available only from October to January makes it that much more precious.

Third is silky-smooth gelato. This frozen dairy dessert has a compact, dense texture thanks to a lower cream content and slower churning speed than plain old ice cream. Gelato's cold caress is particularly suited to summer, but its intense flavors deserve to be enjoyed year-round.

Fourth on the list, and best of all, is gianduja, a northern Italian delicacy born of necessity when Napoleon embargoed cocoa exports in the early nineteenth century.

Gianduja was invented to stretch the small amount of cocoa powder available with ground hazelnuts. More than two centuries later, only a handful of these chocolatiers, known as gianduiere, work in Turin's historic labs. There, they create the rich delicacy by hand, with pride in their craft and joy in handling of the precious ingredients.

It is very much like the feelings that Maribel the chocolatier expresses when she talks of how she blends her ganache, and envisions ever more beautiful chocolate confections.

Opposite: A line of clothes air-drying in the morning sun.

DINING
BY THE LAKE

Lake Como needs no introduction. Situated near the city of Milan, it is home to spectacular scenery, beautiful old villas, and historic hotels. Its timeless appeal as an elite travel destination blossomed in the 1700s, when aristocrats, intellectuals, and the members of wealthy families began to embark on the Grand Tour—a voyage to see the great classical sights of Italy considered the final step in acquiring an education and refined taste.

Opposite: *A table in a splendid lakeshore garden offers the utmost in tranquility.*

Veal Meatballs
with Lemon Sauce

These tender meatballs in a creamy, lemony sauce are audaciously good and perfect for any occasion—from an intimate lunch to a dinner for many. The sauce is tasty and not too rich, with the zing of lemon balancing the richness of the cream.

• SERVES 4 •

MEATBALLS

2 slices day-old bread, crusts removed

½ cup (120 ml) whole milk

1 pound (455 g) ground veal, or a mixture of veal, pork, and beef

1 large egg, beaten

¼ cup (25 g) grated Parmigiano Reggiano

¼ cup (15 g) chopped flat-leaf parsley leaves

1 clove garlic, minced

Pinch freshly grated nutmeg

1½ teaspoons (7.5 g) kosher salt

Freshly ground black pepper

All-purpose flour, for dredging

Extra-virgin olive oil, for pan-frying

2 cups (480 ml) chicken broth

Lemon slices, for garnish

SAUCE

2 tablespoons (30 ml) extra-virgin olive oil

½ medium white onion, minced

2 tablespoons (15 g) all-purpose flour

1 cup (240 ml) heavy cream

Grated zest and juice of 1 small lemon

Kosher salt and freshly ground black pepper

Preheat the oven to 350°F/175°C.

For the meatballs, tear the bread into chunks and put in a small bowl. Pour the milk over the bread and allow to rest until the bread is soaked and softened. Squeeze the bread by hand and crumble it into a large bowl. (Discard the milk.) To the bread, add the veal, egg, Parmigiano, parsley, garlic, nutmeg, salt, and a generous amount of pepper. Knead by hand to combine. Form into eight 1-inch (2.5-cm) meatballs and set on a plate.

Spread some flour in a shallow bowl for dredging. In a skillet large enough to hold the meatballs in a single layer, heat a thin film of olive oil over medium heat. Dredge the meatballs in flour, then add to the skillet and brown on all sides, about 5 minutes. Pour in the broth, bring to a simmer, and cover the skillet. Simmer, covered, until the meatballs are just cooked through, 10 to 15 minutes. Remove the meatballs to a baking sheet and place in the oven to crisp up while you make the sauce. Strain the meatball cooking liquid, reserving 1 cup (240 ml). Discard excess, or add water if necessary to have enough liquid.

For the sauce, heat the olive oil in a medium saucepan over medium-low heat. Add the onion and cook until soft but not taking on color, about 5 minutes. Sprinkle with the flour and cook, stirring, just until the flour smells a little nutty but is not turning brown, about 1 minute. Whisk in the reserved meatball cooking juices and the cream and bring to a simmer. Cook until the sauce is thickened, 5 to 7 minutes. Whisk in the lemon zest and juice and remove from the heat. Season with salt and pepper.

To serve, arrange the meatballs on a warm platter and spoon the sauce over them. Grind some black pepper on top. Garnish with lemon slices and serve.

Above, left to right: A traditional Italian village street; a lounge chair and a view of Lake Como; the crenelated tower of the Castle of Rezzonico on the shores of Lake Como.

ON THE SANTA MARGHERITA SHORE

Santa Margherita Ligure is a stunning port and resort town in Liguria. It sits in a protected bay on one of the most beautiful stretches of the Riviera di Ponente. Destroyed, rebuilt, and then conquered several times by Saracen pirates, today it is a waterside gem just two miles from bustling Portofino.

__Opposite:__ Whether in winter by a roaring fire or in summer on a terrace by the sea, a molten chocolate cake (page 29) and a grapefruit-infused cocktail (page 228) are a perfect combination.

Grapefruit Cocktail

The tangy combination of gin and grapefruit juice is a global favorite. Swap in vodka for the gin and you've got a greyhound.

• 1 SERVING •

1 cup (240 g) ice, plus more for serving

1 ounce (30 ml) Campari

1 ounce (30 ml) gin

2 ounces (60 ml) pink grapefruit juice

2 ounces (60 ml) club soda

Orange slice or sprig of mint, for garnish

Fill a cocktail shaker with ice. Add the Campari, gin, grapefruit juice, and club soda and shake well.

Fill a cocktail glass with ice. Strain the drink into the glass.

Garnish with an orange slice or a sprig of mint.

Insalata Nizzarda

Italy's Liguria region, whose culinary traditions overlap with those in the South of France, has its own version of a Niçoise salad (see recipe, page 128), known as insalata nizzarda.

• SERVES 6 TO 8 •

Kosher salt

9 new potatoes, about 1 pound (455 g)

2 pounds (1 kg) haricots verts, blanched

½ cup (120 g) pitted green Ligurian olives

½ cup (120 g) caperberries, stemmed and halved

1 teaspoon (5 g) coarsely ground black pepper

¾ cup (180 ml) Champagne Vinaigrette or White Wine Vinaigrette (see recipe, page 128)

1 head bibb lettuce, leaves separated and left whole

6 hard-boiled eggs, peeled and quartered lengthwise

10 plum tomatoes, halved

One 12-ounce (340-g) jar oil-packed anchovy fillets, drained

Bring a large pot of salted water to a boil and cook the potatoes until tender enough to pierce with a paring knife, 10 to 12 minutes. Drain and set aside to cool. When the potatoes are cool enough to handle, peel and slice them and place the slices in a large bowl.

Add the haricots verts, olives, caperberries, 1 teaspoon (5 g) salt, and the pepper. Pour the vinaigrette over the vegetables and toss gently.

Line a platter with the lettuce leaves. Place the potato mixture in the center, and position the egg wedges and tomatoes around the perimeter. Place the anchovies on top of the potatoes. Serve at room temperature.

Focaccia
with Ricotta & Prosciutto Cotto

Choose between this savory focaccia or the following sweet one, or offer your guests one of each, as they complement each other. The name focaccia derives from the Latin *panis focacius*; the recipe for this popular flatbread varies from region to region, though Liguria is most closely associated with it.

• SERVES 4 •

1 cup (240 g) ricotta

Grated zest of ½ lemon

One 8-inch (20-cm) square plain focaccia, about 1 inch (2.5 cm) thick

¾ cup (170 g) diced prosciutto cotto

Extra-virgin olive oil, for drizzling

Flaky sea salt, for sprinkling

Preheat the oven to 425°F/220°C with a rack in the lower third. Stir together the ricotta and lemon zest in a small bowl. Place the focaccia on a baking sheet. Dollop the ricotta on top of the focaccia. Sprinkle on the prosciutto cotto. Drizzle with olive oil and season with flaky salt.

Bake until the focaccia is hot and the bottom and edges are crisp, 10 to 12 minutes. Cut into small squares to serve.

Focaccia
with Walnuts, Figs & Honey

On a terrace by the sea a long-ago pairing lives. Both figs and walnuts were important foods in ancient Greco-Roman culture. The fig was associated with fertility, while the walnut was thought to be a favorite of the god Jupiter.

• SERVES 4 •

One 8-inch (20-cm) square plain focaccia, about 1 inch (2.5 cm) thick

4 dried black figs, soaked in water to soften, then drained and coarsely chopped

½ cup (50 g) walnuts

½ teaspoon (1 g) fresh thyme leaves

Extra-virgin olive oil, for drizzling

Flaky sea salt, for sprinkling

Honey, for drizzling

Preheat the oven to 425°F/220°C with a rack in the lower third. Place the focaccia on a baking sheet. Sprinkle with the figs, walnuts, and thyme. Drizzle with olive oil and sprinkle with flaky salt.

Bake until the focaccia is hot and the bottom and edges are crisp, 10 to 12 minutes. Drizzle with honey and cut into small squares to serve.

MARIBEL'S WORLD

Maribel's world of sweet confections is one of pure magic and boundless joy. The fruit of her imagination has been shaped by her Honduran heritage, distilled from a lifetime of travel and adventures, and nourished by the love of family.

The decorative accents of MarieBelle chocolate creations express her joie de vivre and her whimsical French style—Maribel's rococo.

From the jewel-box interiors of the MarieBelle shops to the ornately designed packaging and artwork that touches everything, every detail is playful, theatrical, and carefully considered.

It's Chocolates
Chocolates
And . . .
More Chocolates
And No Passport Needed!

This is Maribel's world.

Acknowledgments

MarieBelle Entertains is a celebration of my Honduran heritage and the many friends and family members who have enriched my life and made my journey possible. First and foremost, I am grateful to my husband, Jacques, and my daughter, Angelina, whom I love beyond words. My deepest gratitude goes to my mother, Bertha de Martinez, for setting an extraordinary example for me with her hard work and perseverance; to my father, Mariano Martinez, for his positive attitude; to my strong sisters, Esmeralda Martinez Haydee de Valle, Lillian Martinez, Thelma Martinez, Lourdes Baide, and Silvia Poveda; to my brother Augusto Martinez; and to the rest of my extended family for their love and support.

A warm thank you to my friend Selima Salaun for believing in me; to my dearest friend, Keiko Aoki; to Prince Dimitri of Yugoslavia for making the introduction to Maria Cristina Rizzo; and to my brother Aguinaldo Martinez for helping me research cacao and its origins. Thanks to my niece Nadia Martinez, whose help in Menorca was beyond anything I could have asked for; to Estefania Murillo, who helped me translate many of the recipes for the home cook; and to my sister Esmeralda, who tested many of the recipes—work so crucial for this cookbook.

I wish to extend my gratitude to Carolina von Humboldt Interiors, Christopher von Hohenberg, Prince Dimitri of Yugoslavia, Robert W. Kean III, and Caroline Gerry for their help with the New York locations. Also, a thank you to Princess Ezurin Khyra for her beautiful flower arrangement, and to Alana Moskowitz at Kravet Fabrics for providing the Lee Joffa tablecloths. For their support in Menorca, Spain, I am grateful to Marin and Damien de Clercq, Victoria Strauss, Natasha and Henri Suarez d'Aulan, Cecilia de Grelle, and Manuel Balbontin. For their gracious hospitality in Italy, I wish to thank Roberta Lamperti, Agriturismo di Mombisaggio, and Castello di Montegioco and Villa Traversi in Laglio, Como. They opened their homes and their kitchens so that we could bring these dishes to life. I also wish to thank Flavia Cuevas at Hacienda San Lucas in Copán, Honduras, for making us feel at home, and Maya Rollin at Château des Alpilles in Saint-Rémy for opening her doors and accommodating us despite her busy schedule, as well as Richard Behmoiras, who welcomed us into his house in Provence, and Han Feng for her kind hospitality in New York City.

This project owes everything to the creative eye and enthusiasm of Maria Cristina Rizzo, who led her team to make an idea into a reality. My thanks to Mark Roskams, for his beautiful and joyful photography. His images shine with the light of my birthplace and bring to life my favorite dishes, the places that I love, and, of course, the chocolates. And many thanks also go to Lavinia Branca Snyder for her research into Lenca history in Honduras and for her eloquent writing. Finally, I would like to extend my appreciation to Natalie Danford for her careful and skilled hand in helping me to craft the language of my recipes.

Finally, I would like to thank Sandy Gilbert for her guidance and sure hand at Rizzoli; Jan Derevjanik for her imaginative design; and, most importantly, to Charles Miers for believing in me. With the support and hard work of the diligent Rizzoli team, *MarieBelle Entertains* has become a beautiful reality.

Biographies

AUTHOR MARIBEL LIEBERMAN, founder and CEO of MarieBelle New York, was born and raised near the cacao fields of Honduras. As a young girl, she made sweets and sold them to the local community. She emigrated to the United States and studied at Parsons School of Design, where she developed her sensibility for luxury goods, fine food, and elegant fashion. Maribel launched her entrepreneurial career in the 1990s with Maribel's Gourmet Cuisine, a catering enterprise serving high-profile clients, such as US diplomats and even President Clinton. Today, after more than two decades, MarieBelle New York has an expanding global presence with two chocolate shops in New York City, including a boutique at the Kitano Hotel; three venues in Japan; and an online store in Hong Kong. Planning is underway to open a new location on Manhattan's Upper East Side this year.

PHOTOGRAPHER MARK ROSKAMS, a native of Australia, started his photography career in the early 1980s when he developed an interest in shooting architecture and design. His work led him from New York to Florida, the Caribbean, and Europe. His photographs have been featured in numerous publications, including *Architectural Digest* editions for Germany, France, Italy, Russia, and China and *Elle Decor*. His Rizzoli books include *Masseria: The Italian Farmhouses of Puglia; Entertaining Chic! Modern French Recipes and Table Settings for All Occasions; Equestrian Life: From Riding Houses to Country Estates; Once Upon a Diamond: A Family Tradition of Royal Jewels;* and *Serafina: Modern Italian Cuisine for Everyday Home Cooking*.

WRITER LAVINIA BRANCA SNYDER is an Italian-born, New York–based writer. Most recently she coauthored *Once Upon a Diamond: A Family Tradition of Royal Jewels; Entertaining Chic! Modern French Recipes and Table Settings for All Occasions; Equestrian Life: From Riding Houses to Country Estates;* and *Serafina: Modern Italian Cuisine for Everyday Home Cooking*. Prior to her Rizzoli projects, she penned a series of children's books: *The Ooshes, Softi's Adventures,* and *The Kyss Family Mysteries*.

ART DIRECTOR MARIA CRISTINA RIZZO has worked in the field of photography for many years, as a talent agent; as a photography gallery owner and curator of photographic exhibitions; and, most recently, as an art director and photo editor. Of Italian descent, Cristina has lived in London and New York, as well as Milan. Her books for Rizzoli include *Masseria: The Italian Farmhouses of Puglia; Inson Dubois Wood: Interiors; Entertaining Chic! Modern French Recipes and Table Settings for All Occasions; Equestrian Life: From Riding Houses to Country Estates; Once Upon a Diamond: A Family Tradition of Royal Jewels;* and *Serafina: Modern Italian Cuisine for Everyday Home Cooking*.

Recipe Index

(Page references in *itallics* refer to illustrations.)

A

Aguilar, Friar Jerónimo de, 158
Alborotos, *44, 45*
almond(s):
  Florentines, 26, *27*
  Orange Flourless Cake with Chocolate Topping, *162, 163*
  Romesco, 62
Álvaro, Abbot Antonio de, 122
anchovies, in Insalata Nizzarda, 228, *229*
Andalusian Migas, *148, 149*
appetizers and starters:
  Citrus & Seafood Escabeche with Red Pepper, 134, *135*
  Clams with Garlic & Wine, 168, *169*
  Grilled Sardines, 156, *157*
  Grilled Shrimp, 156, *157*
  Salmon Tartare with Cilantro, 100, *101*
  Stuffed Artichokes, *196, 197*
  Supplì, *212, 213*
  Tiradito with Chiles & Citrus Dressing, 100, *101*
  see also tapas
Asparagus, Roasted, with Chopped Egg, 182, *183*
Aztec Hot Chocolate, MarieBelle, American style and European style, 18, *19*
Aztecs, 10, 56

B

Bacon, Pork Loin Stuffed with Prunes, Walnuts &, 92, *93*
Baguette with Melted Chocolate & Fresh Lavender Butter, *94, 95*
Basilica of Our Lady of the Pillar, Zaragoza, Spain, *123*
Basmati Rice with Cilantro, Dill & Potatoes, 68
Beans, Blended, My Way, 71
beef:
  Seared Filet Mignon with Roasted Maitake Mushrooms & Fennel, 114, *115*
  Short Ribs with Chocolate Sauce, Jacques's, 190, *191*

Tapado Olanchano (Honduran Beef Stew), 74, *75*
Beet Puree, 104, *105*
Beignets, Orange, with Powdered Sugar, *198, 199*
bistronomy, 186
Blended Beans My Way, 71
Branzino (or Corvina), Fried, 52, 53
bread(s):
  Baguette with Melted Chocolate & Fresh Lavender Butter, *94, 95*
  Coca de Vidre (Glass Flatbread), *170, 171*
  cubes, dried, in Andalusian Migas, *148, 149*
  Focaccia with Ricotta & Prosciutto Cotto, 230, *231*
  Focaccia with Walnuts, Figs & Honey, 230, 231
  Pan de Coco, 60, *60*
breakfast, Honduran (A Garden Breakfast menu), 36, 40–47, *41*
  Alborotos, *44, 45*
  Hojuelas, 46, *47*
  Plantains, Fried Ripe, 42, *43*
  Sweet Corn Pancakes, 46, *47*
  Tropical Fruit Salad, 42, *43*
brunch (New York Sunday Brunch menu), 78, 82–85, *83*
  Crêpes Suzette, 84, *105*
Butter, Fresh Lavender, *94, 95*
butternut squash, in Roasted Root Vegetables, 95

C

cacahuatl, 10
cacao:
  history of, 9–13, 122, 158
  Lancan myths about, 9–10
  Mesoamerican beverages made with, 9–11, *10*
  processed into cocoa, 12
  Theobroma, 11, *11*, 13
cacao, origin of word, 10
cacao pods, 12, *13*, 38
  cutting, 64
cacao tree, 10, 39
Cadaqués, Spain, 166–67, *166–173*
cakes:
  Flourless Chocolate, Dimitri's, 30, *31*

Flourless Orange-Almond, with Chocolate Topping, *162, 163*
  Ganache, Marie Antoinette, *32, 33*
  Molten Chocolate, 28, 29, *227*
Caprese Salad with Currants, Strawberries & Tomatoes, 182, *184*
carrots, in Roasted Root Vegetables, 95
Champagne Vinaigrette, 128
Cheese & Corn Dumpling Soup (Sopa de Capirotadas), 50, *51*
cherries, dried, in Florentines, 26, *27*
Cherry Tomatoes, Sautéed, 88, *89*
Chimichurri, 52
chocolate:
  -dipped corn ball (Alborotos), *44, 45*
  Drizzle, Cinnamon-Infused Churros with, 124, *125*
  health benefits of, 13
  history of, 9–13, 122, 158
  Hojuelas drizzled with, 46, *47*
  Melted, Baguette with Fresh Lavender Butter &, *94, 95*
  Melted Dark, for Dipping, 124, *185*
  Sauce, Jacques's Short Ribs with, 190, *191*
  Topping, Flourless Orange-Almond Cake with, *162, 163*
  white, in Matcha Truffles, 22, *23*
chocolate creations, 16–33
  Chocolate-Covered Toffee Bites, 24, *25*
  Dark Chocolate Truffles, 20, *21*
  Florentines, 26, *27*
  Flourless Chocolate Cake, Dimitri's, 30, *31*
  Hot Chocolate, MarieBelle's, 18, *19*
  Marie Antoinette Ganache Cake, *32, 33*
  Matcha Truffles, 22, *23*
  Molten Chocolate Cakes, 28, 29, *227*
  see also chocolates, MarieBelle
chocolate drinks:
  first European encounters with, in New World, 158
  first made in Europe, 11, 122
  Hot Chocolate, MarieBelle's, 18, *19*
  ingredients and implements for, *159*
  Mesoamerican, 9–11, *10*
chocolates, MarieBelle, 12, 14–15, *106–7*, 232, *233*

cacao pods prepared for, 12
decorated with Jacques Lieberman's painting motifs, 96, *97*, *187*
with designs celebrating Statue of Liberty, *81*
chorizo, in Tapado Olanchano (Honduran Beef Stew), 74, *75*
Chowder, Conch (Sopa de Caracol Conch Chowder), 55
Churros, Cinnamon-Infused, with Chocolate Drizzle, 124, *125*
cilantro, in Chimichurri, 52
Cinnamon-Infused Churros with Chocolate Drizzle, 124, *125*
Cistercian Monastery of Our Lady of Stone, near Zaragoza, Spain, *122*
citrus:
  -Infused Fish Fillet with Grilled Tomatillos & Arugula Sprouts, *112, 113*
  & Seafood Escabeche with Red Pepper, 134, *135*
Clams with Garlic & Wine, 168, *169*
Coca de Vidre (Glass Flatbread), *170*, 171
cocktails:
  Cucumber & Tequila, 110, *111*
  Grapefruit, *227*, 228
  Skinny Margarita, 110, *111*
cocoa butter, 12
cocoa nibs, 12
cocoa powder:
  cacao processed into, 12
  Polenta with, *207, 208, 209*
  in savory dishes, 206
  see also cacao
coconut milk:
  Pan de Coco, 60, *60*
  Sopa de Caracol (Conch Chowder), 55
Codex Tudela, 10, *10*
Columbus, Christopher, 11, 158
conch, 57
  Sopa de Caracol (Conch Chowder), 55
Conchagua, 56
cookies: Florentines, 26, *27*
corn:
  ball, chocolate-dipped (Alborotos), *44, 45*

& Cheese Dumpling Soup (Sopa
   de Capirotadas), 50, 51
Sweet, Pancakes, 46, 47
see also masa harina
Cortés, Hernán, 11, 158
corvina:
   Citrus & Seafood Escabeche
      with Red Pepper, 134, 135
   Fried, 52, 53
cotija, in Sopa de Capirotadas (Cheese
   & Corn Dumpling Soup), 50, 51
creation myth, Honduran, 9
Crema Catalana con Ananas, 172, 173
Crêpes Suzette, 84, 105
cucumber:
   & Tequila Cocktail, 110, 111
   & Tomato Salad, 72, 74
Currants, Caprese Salad with
   Strawberries, Tomatoes
   and, 182, 184

D
de las Casas, Friar Bartolomé, 158
desserts:
   Baguette with Melted Chocolate &
      Fresh Lavender Butter, 94, 95
   Cinnamon-Infused Churros with
      Chocolate Drizzle, 124, 125
   Crema Catalana con Ananas, 172, 173
   Figs, Caramelized, 162, 162
   Melted Dark Chocolate for
      Dipping, 124, 185
   Orange Beignets with
      Powdered Sugar, 198, 199
   see also cakes; chocolate creations;
      MarieBelle chocolates
Dining by the Lake menu,
   202, 220–23, 221
Dining in Locust Valley menu,
   78, 98–105, 99
Dining with Legends menu,
   118, 166–73, 167
Dinner in Provence menu,
   176, 188–89, 188–93
Dorado, Grilled Pineapple &,
   with Cilantro, 136, 137
dressings:
   Walnut, 152
   see also vinaigrettes
drinks, see chocolate drinks; cocktails
duck:
   Breast, Roasted, 102, 103
   Confit, Picadito of, with
      Prunes, 140, 141
Dumpling Soup, Cheese & Corn
   (Sopa de Capirotadas), 50, 51

E
egg(s):
   Chopped, Roasted Asparagus
      with, 182, 183
   Ensalada Nizarda, 128, 129
   Insalata Nizzarda, 228, 229
   Zucchini & Potato Tortilla, 146, 147
eggplant:
   Fried, with Honey, 148, 149
   Provençal Ratatouille Tian, 192, 193
Endive & Fig Salad, 152, 153
Ensalada Nizarda, 128, 129
Escabeche, Citrus & Seafood,
   with Red Pepper, 134, 135

F
A Feast of Many Colors menu,
   176, 194–95, 194–99
Fennel & Maitake Mushrooms, Roasted,
   Seared Filet Mignon with, 114, 115
fig(s):
   Caramelized, 162, 162
   & Endive Salad, 152, 153
   Focaccia with Walnuts,
      Honey &, 230, 231
   with Melted Dark Chocolate
      for Dipping, 185
Filet Mignon, Seared, with
   Roasted Maitake Mushrooms
   & Fennel, 114, 115
fish and seafood:
   Citrus & Seafood Escabeche
      with Red Pepper, 134, 135
   Clams with Garlic & Wine, 168, 169
   Corvina, Fried, 52, 53
   Dorado & Pineapple, Grilled,
      with Cilantro, 136, 137
   A Fisherman's Feast menu,
      118, 150–57, 151
   Fish Fillet, Citrus-Infused,
      with Grilled Tomatillos &
      Arugula Sprouts, 112, 113
   Romesco to serve with, 62
   Salmon Tartare with Cilantro, 100, 101
   Sardines, Grilled, 156, 157
   Sea Bass, Sautéed, with Spinach
      and Sauce Verte, 88, 89
   Shrimp, Grilled, 156, 157
   Shrimp & Pineapple Salad, 142, 143
   Sopa de Caracol (Conch
      Chowder), 55
   Tiradito with Chiles & Citrus
      Dressing, 100, 101
   tuna, in Ensalada Nizarda, 128, 129
   tuna, in Pan Bagnat
      Sandwiches, 60, 61
   tuna, in Stuffed Tomatoes, 154, 155

A Fisherman's Feast menu,
   118, 150 57, 151
Florentines, 26, 27
flourless cakes:
   Chocolate, Dimitri's, 30, 31
   Orange-Almond, with Chocolate
      Topping, 162, 163
focaccia, 218
   with Ricotta & Prosciutto
      Cotto, 230, 231
   with Walnuts, Figs & Honey, 230, 231
French cuisine, 174–99
   classique, nouvelle cuisine, and
      bistronomy styles of, 186
   figs served with Melted Dark
      Chocolate for Dipping, 185
   Marie Antoinette Ganache
      Cake, 32, 33
   Orange Beignets with
      Powdered Sugar, 198, 199
   Potatoes with Herb Butter, 196, 196
   Provençal Ratatouille Tian, 192, 193
   Roasted Asparagus with
      Chopped Egg, 182, 183
   Short Ribs with Chocolate
      Sauce, Jacques's, 190, 191
French menus:
   Dinner in Provence, 176,
      188–89, 188–93
   A Feast of Many Colors,
      176, 194–95, 194–99
   A Light Supper in the Shade
      of a Grande Allée, 176,
      180–85, 181, 184–85
fried:
   Corvina, 52, 53
   Eggplant with Honey, 148, 149
   Orange Beignets with
      Powdered Sugar, 198, 199
   Plantains, Ripe, 42, 43
   Supplì, 212, 213
   Yuca Fritters with Grated Tomato
      Sauce & Romesco, 62, 63
fritters:
   Honduran (Hojuelas), 46, 47
   Romesco to serve with, 62
   Yuca, with Grated Tomato
      Sauce & Romesco, 62, 63
Fruit Salad, Tropical, 42, 43

G
Ganache Cake, Marie
   Antoinette, 32, 33
A Garden Breakfast menu,
   36, 40–47, 41
gelato, 218
gianduja, 218

Glass Flatbread (Coca de
   Vidre), 170, 171
Grapefruit Cocktail, 227, 228
Grated Tomato Sauce, 71
grilled:
   Dorado & Pineapple with
      Cilantro, 136, 137
   Sardines, 156, 157
   Shrimp, 156, 157
   Tomatillos, 112, 113

H
haricots verts:
   Ensalada Nizarda, 128, 129
   Insalata Nizzarda, 228, 229
Hojuelas, 46, 47
Honduran cacao producers, 12
Honduran cuisine, 34–75
   Alborotos, 44, 45
   Basmati Rice with Cilantro,
      Dill & Potatoes, 68
   Beans, Blended, My Way, 71
   Chimichurri, 52
   Cucumber & Tomato Salad, 72, 74
   Fried Corvina, 52, 53
   Fried Ripe Plantains, 42, 43
   Grated Tomato Sauce, 71
   Hojuelas, 46, 47
   Pan Bagnat Sandwiches, 60, 61
   Pan de Coco, 60, 60
   Red Cabbage & Onion Salad, 50, 50
   Sopa de Capirotadas (Cheese &
      Corn Dumpling Soup), 50, 51
   Sopa de Caracol (Conch
      Chowder), 55
   Sweet Corn Pancakes, 46, 47
   Tapado Olanchano (Beef
      Stew), 74, 75
   Tropical Fruit Salad, 42, 43
   Vegetarian Pupusas, 72, 73
   Yuca Fritters with Grated Tomato
      Sauce & Romesco, 62, 63
Honduran menus:
   A Garden Breakfast, 36, 40–47, 41
   An Island Lunch, 36, 47–55, 48
   Picnic by the Beach, 36, 58–63, 59
   Tropical Harvest Supper,
      36, 66–75, 67
Hot Chocolate, MarieBelle's, 18, 19

I
Insalata Nizzarda, 228, 229
An Island Lunch menu, 36, 47–55, 48
Italian cuisine, 200–231
   Caprese Salad with Currants,
      Strawberries & Tomatoes, 182, 184

Italian cuisine (cont.)
  Focaccia with Ricotta &
    Prosciutto Cotto, 230, 231
  Focaccia with Walnuts, Figs
    & Honey, 230, 231
  Grapefruit Cocktail, 227, 228
  Insalata Nizzarda, 228, 229
  Osso Buco, 216, 217
  Polenta al Forno, 214, 215
  Polenta with Cocoa Powder,
    207, 208, 209
  Supplì, 212, 213
  Veal Meatballs with Lemon
    Sauce, 222, 223
Italian menus:
  Dining by the Lake, 202, 220–23, 221
  On the Santa Margherita
    Shore, 202, 226–31, 227
  A Table with a View, 202, 210–17, 211
  The Time Traveler, 202, 206–9, 207

L
Lake Como, 220, 220–21
A Late Summer Celebration
  menu, 118, 132–37, 133
Lavender Butter, Fresh, Baguette
  with Melted Chocolate &, 94, 95
Lenca people and language, 9–10, 56
Lieberman, Jacques, 96, 175, 186, 190
  MarieBelle chocolates decorated
    with painting motifs by, 96, 97, 187
A Light Supper in the Shade of
  a Grande Allée menu, 176,
  180–85, 181, 184–85
Linnaeus, Carl, 11
A Lofty Meal menu, 78, 86–89, 87
Lohrentz, Tlm, 56
lunch menus:
  An Island Lunch, 36, 47–55, 48
  Lunch on a Terrace, 78, 90–95, 91

M
Mahi Mahi (Dorado), Grilled Pineapple
  &, with Cilantro, 136, 137
main courses:
  Duck Breast, Roasted, 102, 103
  Filet Mignon, Seared, with
    Roasted Maitake Mushrooms
    & Fennel, 114, 115
  Osso Buco, 216, 217
  Pork Loin Stuffed with Prunes,
    Walnuts & Bacon, 92, 93
  Sea Bass, Sautéed, with Spinach
    and Sauce Verte, 88, 89
  Short Ribs with Chocolate
    Sauce, Jacques's, 190, 191

Tapado Olanchano (Beef
  Stew), 74, 75
Veal Meatballs with Lemon
  Sauce, 222, 223
Maitake Mushrooms & Fennel, Roasted,
  Seared Filet Mignon with, 114, 115
mango, in Tropical Fruit Salad, 42, 43
Margarita, Skinny, 110, 111
Marie Antoinette Ganache Cake, 32, 33
MarieBelle chocolates, 14–15,
  106–7, 232, 233
  cacao pods prepared for, 12
  decorated with Jacques Lieberman's
    painting motifs, 96, 97, 187
  with designs celebrating
    Statue of Liberty, 81
MarieBelle shop in SoHo, New York,
  14–15, 15, 81, 97, back endpaper
masa harina:
  Sopa de Capirotadas (Cheese &
    Corn Dumpling Soup), 50, 51
  Vegetarian Pupusas, 72, 73
Matcha Truffles, 22, 23
Mayans, 9, 9, 10, 10, 11, 66
Meatballs, Veal, with Lemon
  Sauce, 222, 223
Médecin, Jacques, 128
Melted Dark Chocolate for
  Dipping, 124, 185
Menorca island, Spain, 118–65,
  119–21, 126–27, 130–31, 138–39,
  144–45, 160–61, 164–65
Mesoamerican cacao
  beverages, 9–11, 10
milk chocolate, making, 12
Molten Chocolate Cakes, 28, 29, 227
mozzarella:
  Caprese Salad with Currants,
    Strawberries & Tomatoes, 182, 184
  Supplì, 212, 213

N
New York menus:
  Dining in Locust Valley,
    78, 98–105, 99
  A Lofty Meal, 78, 86–89, 87
  Lunch on a Terrace, 78, 90–95, 91
  New York Sunday Brunch,
    78, 82–85, 83, 85
  A White Satin Evening,
    78, 108–9, 108–15
Niçoise salads:
  Ensalada Nizarda, 128, 129
  Insalata Nizzarda, 228, 229
nouvelle cuisine, 186

O
Of Chocolate and Traditions
  menu, 118, 122–25, 125
Of Tapas and Menorca menu,
  118, 144–49, 145
Olmecs, 10, 56
onion(s):
  & Red Cabbage Salad, 50, 50
  Tortilla Española, 154, 156
  VIdalia, in Roasted Root
    Vegetables, 95
On the Santa Margherita Shore
  menu, 202, 226–31, 227
orange:
  Almond Flourless Cake with
    Chocolate Topping, 162, 163
  Beignets with Powdered
    Sugar, 198, 199
  peel, candied, in Florentines, 26, 27
Osso Buco, 216, 217

P
Pan Bagnat Sandwiches, 60, 61
pancakes:
  Sweet Corn, 46, 47
  Vegetarian Pupusas, 72, 73
Pan de Coco, 60, 60
papaya, in Tropical Fruit Salad, 42, 43
Parmigiano Reggiano:
  Sopa de Capirotadas (Cheese &
    Corn Dumpling Soup), 50, 51
  Supplì, 212, 213
parsley, in Chimichurri, 52
Picadito of Duck Confit with
  Prunes, 140, 141
Picnic by the Beach menu,
  36, 58–63, 59
Picnic for an Afternoon Sail
  menu, 118, 138–43, 139
pineapple:
  Crema Catalana con Ananas, 172, 173
  Grilled Dorado &, with
    Cilantro, 136, 137
  & Shrimp Salad, 142, 143
  Tropical Fruit Salad, 42, 43
plantains, ripe:
  Fried, 42, 43
  Tapado Olanchano (Honduran
    Beef Stew), 74, 75
polenta:
  with Cocoa Powder, 207, 208, 209
  al Forno, 214, 215
popcorn, in Alborotos, 44, 45
pork:
  Loin Stuffed with Prunes,
    Walnuts & Bacon, 92, 93

ribs and chicharrones, in
  Tapado Olanchano (Honduran
    Beef Stew), 74, 75
rinds, in Andalusian Migas, 148, 149
potato(es):
  Ensalada Nizarda, 128, 129
  with Herb Butter, 196, 196
  Insalata Nizzarda, 228, 229
  Roasted Root Vegetables, 95
  Tortilla Española, 154, 156
  & Zucchini Tortilla, 146, 147
Prosciutto Cotto, Focaccia with
  Ricotta and, 230, 231
Provençal cuisine, 174–99
  Dinner in Provence menu,
    176, 188–89, 188–93
  A Feast of Many Colors menu,
    176, 194–95, 194–99
  Ratatouille Tian, 192, 193
prunes:
  Picadito of Duck Confit with, 140, 141
  Pork Loin Stuffed with
    Walnuts, Bacon &, 92, 93
Pupusas, Vegetarian, 72, 73

Q
queso fresco, in Sopa de
  Capirotadas (Cheese & Corn
  Dumpling Soup), 50, 51
Quetzalcoatl, 10, 10, 56

R
Ratatouille Tian, Provençal, 192, 193
Red Cabbage & Onion Salad, 50, 50
red peppers, in Romesco, 62
rice:
  Basmati, with Cilantro,
    Dill & Potatoes, 68
  flour, in Vegetarian Pupusas, 72, 73
  Supplì, 212, 213
Ricotta, Focaccia with Prosciutto
  Cotto &, 230, 231
Romesco, 62
Root Vegetables, Roasted, 95

S
Saint-Rémy-de-Provence, France,
  176–99, 177–79, 184–85
salads:
  Caprese, with Currants, Strawberries
    & Tomatoes, 182, 184
  Cucumber & Tomato, 72, 74
  Endive & Fig, 152, 153
  Ensalada Nizarda, 128, 129
  Insalata Nizzarda, 228, 229
  Red Cabbage & Onion, 50, 50
  Shrimp & Pineapple, 142, 143

Tropical Fruit, 42, 43
Salmon Tartare with Cilantro, 100, *101*
Sandwiches, Pan Bagnat, 60, 61
Santa Margherita, Liguria, Italy,
 204-5, 226-27, 226-31, 230
Sardines, Grilled, 156, *157*
sauces:
 Chimichurri, 52
 Grated Tomato, 71
 Romesco, 62
Sauce Verte, 88
scallops, in Citrus & Seafood
 Escabeche with Red
 Pepper, 134, *135*
sea bass:
 Citrus-Infused Fish Fillet
 with Grilled Tomatillos &
 Arugula Sprouts, *112*, 113
 Citrus & Seafood Escabeche
 with Red Pepper, 134, *135*
 Sautéed, with Spinach and
 Sauce Verte, 88, *89*
Short Ribs with Chocolate
 Sauce, Jacques's, 190, *191*
shrimp:
 Citrus & Seafood Escabeche
 with Red Pepper, 134, *135*
 Grilled, 156, *157*
 & Pineapple Salad, *142*, 143
 Sopa de Caracol (Conch
 Chowder), 55
side dishes:
 Asparagus, Roasted, with
 Chopped Egg, 182, *183*
 Basmati Rice with Cilantro,
 Dill & Potatoes, 68
 Beans, Blended, My Way, 71
 Beet Puree, 104, *105*
 Cherry Tomatoes, Sautéed, 88, *89*
 Eggplant, Fried, with Honey, *148*, 149
 Figs, Caramelized, 162, *162*
 Maitake Mushrooms &
 Fennel, Roasted, 114, *115*
 Polenta al Forno, *214*, 215
 Potatoes with Herb Butter, 196, *196*
 Provençal Ratatouille Tian, *192*, 193
 Root Vegetables, Roasted, 95
 Stuffed Artichokes, 196, *197*
 Sweet Potato Chips, Roasted, 115, *115*
 Tomatillos, Grilled, *112*, 113
Siraudin, Paul, 33
skewers:
 Grilled Dorado & Pineapple
 with Cilantro, 136, *137*
 Grilled Sardines, 156, *157*
 Grilled Shrimp, 156, *157*
Skinny Margarita, 110, *111*

Sofrito, 113
Sopa de Capirotadas (Cheese &
 Corn Dumpling Soup), 50, *51*
Sopa de Caracol (Conch Chowder), 55
Spanish cuisine, 116-73
 Andalusian Migas, *148*, 149
 Caramelized Figs, 162, *162*
 Cinnamon-Infused Churros with
 Chocolate Drizzle, 124, *125*
 Citrus & Seafood Escabeche
 with Red Pepper, 134, *135*
 Clams with Garlic & Wine, 168, *169*
 Coca de Vidre (Glass
 Flatbread), *170*, 171
 Crema Catalana con Ananas, 172, *173*
 Endive & Fig Salad, 152, *153*
 Ensalada Nizarda, 128, *129*
 Flourless Orange-Almond Cake
 with Chocolate Topping, 162, *163*
 Fried Eggplant with Honey, *148*, 149
 Grilled Dorado & Pineapple
 with Cilantro, 136, *137*
 Grilled Sardines, 156, *157*
 Grilled Shrimp, 156, *157*
 Picadito of Duck Confit
 with Prunes, 140, *141*
 Romesco, 62
 Shrimp & Pineapple Salad, *142*, 143
 Stuffed Tomatoes, *154*, 155
 Tortilla Española, *154*, 156
 Zucchini & Potato Tortilla, 146, *147*
Spanish menus:
 Dining with Legends, 118, 166-73, *167*
 A Fisherman's Feast, 118, 150-57, *151*
 A Late Summer Celebration,
 118, 132-37, *133*
 Of Chocolate and Traditions,
 118, 122-25, *125*
 Of Tapas and Menorca,
 118, 144-49, *145*
 Picnic for an Afternoon
 Sail, 118, 138-43, *139*
 A Sunset Supper, 118, 160-65, *164-65*
 Within White Walls, 118, 126-29, *129*
Spinach, Sautéed Sea Bass with,
 and Sauce Verte, 88, *89*
Stew, Beef, Honduran (Tapado
 Olanchano), 74, 75
Strawberries, Caprese Salad with
 Currants, Tomatoes &, 182, *184*
Stuffed Artichokes, 196, *197*
Stuffed Tomatoes, *154*, 155
A Sunset Supper menu, 118,
 160-65, *164-65*
Supplì, 212, *213*
Sweet Corn Pancakes, 46, *47*
sweet potato(es):

Chips, Roasted, 115, *115*
Roasted Root Vegetables, 95

T
A Table with a View menu,
 202, 210-17, *211*
Tapado Olanchano (Honduran
 Beef Stew), 74, 75
tapas, 139, 145
 Andalusian Migas, *148*, 149
 Fried Eggplant with Honey, *148*, 149
 Of Tapas and Menorca
 menu, 118, 144-49, *145*
 Picadito of Duck Confit
 with Prunes, 140, *141*
 Stuffed Tomatoes, *154*, 155
 Tortilla Española, *154*, 156
 Zucchini & Potato Tortilla, 146, *147*
Tequila & Cucumber Cocktail, 110, *111*
Theobroma cacao, 11, *11*, 13
The Time Traveler menu,
 202, 206-9, *207*
Tiradito with Chiles & Citrus
 Dressing, 100, *101*
Toffee Bites, Chocolate-
 Covered, 24, 25
Toltecs, 10
Tomatillos, Grilled, *112*, 113
tomato(es):
 Caprese Salad with Currants,
 Strawberries &, 182, *184*
 Cherry, Sautéed, 88, *89*
 & Cucumber Salad, 72, *74*
 Grated, Sauce, 71
 Romesco, 62
 Stuffed, *154*, 155
 Tortilla, Zucchini & Potato, 146, *147*
 Tortilla Española, *154*, 156
 Tropical Fruit Salad, 42, *43*
Tropical Harvest Supper
 menu, 36, 66-75, *67*
truffles, 13
 Dark Chocolate, *20*, 21
 Matcha, 22, *23*
truffles, white, 218
tuna:
 Ensalada Nizarda, 128, *129*
 Pan Bagnat Sandwiches, 60, 61
 Stuffed Tomatoes, *154*, 155
turnips, in Roasted Root Vegetables, 95

V
veal:
 Meatballs with Lemon
 Sauce, 222, *223*
 Osso Buco, 216, *217*
Vegetarian Pupusas, 72, *73*

vinaigrettes:
 Champagne or White Wine, 128
 Simple, 143

W
walnut(s):
 Dressing, 152
 Focaccia with Figs, Honey &, *230*, 231
watermelon, in Tropical
 Fruit Salad, 42, *43*
white chocolate, in Matcha
 Truffles, 22, *23*
white fish:
 Citrus-Infused Fish Fillet
 with Grilled Tomatillos &
 Arugula Sprouts, *112*, 113
 Sopa de Caracol (Conch
 Chowder), 55
 Tiradito with Chiles & Citrus
 Dressing, 100, *101*
A White Satin Evening menu,
 78, 108-9, 108-15
White Wine Vinaigrette, 128
Within White Walls menu,
 118, 126-29, *129*

X
xocolatl, 10, *10*

Y
yuca:
 Fritters with Grated Tomato
 Sauce & Romesco, 62, *63*
 Sopa de Caracol (Conch
 Chowder), 55
 Tapado Olanchano (Honduran
 Beef Stew), *74*, 75

Z
zucchini:
 & Potato Tortilla, 146, *147*
 Provençal Ratatouille Tian, *192*, 193

First published in the United States of America in 2024 by
Rizzoli International Publications, Inc.
300 Park Avenue South
New York, NY 10010
www.rizzoliusa.com

Text by Lavinia Branca Snyder
Photography by Mark Roskams
Art Direction by Maria Cristina Rizzo

OTHER CREDITS
Page 10 (top): Drawing of a Maya woman preparing a chocolate
drink, from the 1553 *Codex Tudela*, Museo de America
Collection, Madrid. The History Collection/Alamy Stock Photo
(bottom, left): Kakau glyph. VVVladimir, public domain
(bottom, right): Quetzalcoatl illustration. iStock.com/Krusto
Page 11: Cacao Theobroma illustration. Quagga Media/Alamy
Stock Photo
Page 15 (left): photograph by Ricardo Rivera
Pages 39 (bottom right) and 186: Maribel Lieberman's
personal archival photographs
Page 158: Bernal Díaz del Castillo, *The True History of the
Conquest of New Spain*, trans. Janet Burke and Ted Humphrey
(Indianapolis: Hackett Publishing Company, 2012)

Publisher: Charles Miers
Project Editor: Sandra Gilbert Freidus
Design: Jan Derevjanik
Production Manager: Kaija Markoe
Managing Editor: Lynn Scrabis
Editorial Assistance: Natalie Danford, Cathy Dorsey,
Caitlin Leffel, Tricia Levi, Amy Stevenson

Printed in China

2024 2025 2026 2027 / 10 9 8 7 6 5 4 3 2 1

ISBN: 978-0-8478-3722-9
Library of Congress Control Number: 2024934475

Visit us online:
Facebook.com/RizzoliNewYork
instagram.com/rizzolibooks
X.com/Rizzoli_Books
pinterest.com/rizzolibooks
youtube.com/user/RizzoliNY

FSC
www.fsc.org
MIX
Paper | Supporting
responsible forestry
FSC® C104723